African art in transit is an absorbing account of the commodification and circulation of African objects in the international art market today. Based on extensive field research among art traders in Côte d'Ivoire, Christopher Steiner analyzes the role of the African middleman in linking those who produce and supply works of art in Africa with those who buy and collect so-called "primitive" art in Europe and America. Moving easily from ethnographic vignette to social theory, Steiner provides a lucid interpretation which reveals not only a complex economic network with its own internal logic and rules, but also an elaborate process of transcultural valuation and exchange. By focusing directly on the intermediaries in the African art trade, he unveils a critical new perspective on how symbolic codes and economic values are produced and mediated in the context of shifting geographic and cultural domains. He calls into question conventional definitions of authenticity in African art, demonstrating how the categories "authentic" and "traditional" are continually negotiated and redefined by a plurality of market participants spread out across the globe.

African art in transit

African art in transit

Christopher B. Steiner

Natural History Museum of Los Angeles County

CAMBRIDGE
UNIVERSITY PRESS

Published by the Press Syndicate of the University of Cambridge
The Pitt Building, Trumpington Street, Cambridge CB2 1RP
40 West 20th Street, New York, NY 10011–4211, USA
10 Stamford Road, Oakleigh, Melbourne 3166, Australia

© Cambridge University Press 1994

First published 1994
Reprinted 1995

Printed in Great Britain at the University Press, Cambridge

A catalogue record for this book is available from the British Library

Library of Congress cataloguing in publication data

ISBN 0 521 43447 5 hardback
ISBN 0 521 45752 1 paperback

WD

For my parents and Kathy
with love and gratitude

Because no idea and no object can exist in isolation from its cultural context, it is impossible to sever mechanically an item from one culture and place it in another. Bronislaw Malinowski, "The Life of Culture" (1927)

A collector we know has placed his primitive art in niches with palm-tree backgrounds. This may be all right for a Lord and Taylor window, but it just doesn't work in a home. Matty Alperton, "Decorating with Primitive Art" (1981)

Contents

List of illustrations   *page* x
Acknowledgments   xiii

    Introduction: The anthropology of African art in a
    transnational market   1

1 Commodity outlets and the classification of goods   16

2 The division of labor and the management of capital   40

3 An economy of words: bargaining and the social production
    of value   61

4 The political economy of ethnicity in a plural market   80

5 The quest for authenticity and the invention of African art   100

6 Cultural brokerage and the mediation of knowledge   130

    Conclusion: African art and the discourses of value   157

Notes   165
References   195
Index   211

Illustrations

Maps

1 Map of Côte d'Ivoire.   *page* 3
2 Map of Abidjan.   22
3 Plan of Plateau market place, Abidjan.   24

Plates

1 Young boys at Plateau market place polishing Senufo masks
  with paste wax. Abidjan, April 1988.   17
2 Market-place stall. Bouaké, December 1987.   20
3 Traders at their stalls in front of Le Mont Korhogo Hotel.
  Korhogo, August 1988.   21
4 Partial view of the inside of an original concrete-frame stall
  at the Plateau market place. Abidjan, June 1988.   23
5 Wooden-frame stall built in the 1970s at the Plateau market
  place. Abidjan, June 1988.   25
6 Storehouse with proprietors. Treichville quarter, Abidjan,
  November 1987.   27
7 Hausa storehouse-owners with children. Treichville quarter,
  Abidjan, July 1988.   29
8 "Marchand d'Objets d'Arts Africains" art gallery and souvenir
  shop outside Hotel Les Cascades. Man, June 1988.   31
9 "Galerie Bassamoise" roadside stall. Near Grand Bassam,
  October 1987.   33
10 Artisanal workshop. Port de Carena, Abidjan, June 1988.   37
11 Dan doll with painted wooden face and costume made of
   cotton cloth, raphia fibers, feathers, wool yarn, and fur.
   Private collection. Photograph by Richard Meier.   43
12 Interior view of an art storehouse. Treichville quarter,
   Abidjan, November 1987.   45
13 Market-place stallholder with his stock of merchandise.
   Man, June 1988.   47

14 European tourists negotiating a sale with Wolof traders at
   Plateau market place. Abidjan, December 1987.   57
15 Hausa trader examining a Senufo statue before offering a price
   to an itinerant supplier. Aoussabougou, Korhogo, December 1987.   63
16 Hausa traders bargaining in a storehouse. Treichville quarter,
   Abidjan, June 1991.   67
17 Senufo *kpélié*-style mask. Private collection. Photograph by
   Richard Meier.   83
18 Wooden house ladders in a trader's storehouse. Treichville
   quarter, Abidjan, June 1991.   113
19 Wooden pestles in a trader's storehouse. Treichville quarter,
   Abidjan, June 1991.   115
20 Slingshots stained with potassium permanganate drying at the
   Plateau market place. Abidjan, March 1988.   116
21 A pile of slingshots displayed among other objects at the stall
   of a Plateau market-place trader. Abidjan, April 1988.   117
22 Carver finishing the detail work on a wooden slingshot.
   Abidjan, March 1988.   118
23 Broken Baule statue "transformed" into a slingshot by replacing
   the broken legs with a forked pinnacle. Abidjan, July 1988.   119
24 Employee at an African art framing gallery constructing a box
   frame for a display of Akan goldweights. Abidjan, July 1991.   121
25 A framed Dan mask and brass bracelet and goldweights on
   display at an African art framing gallery. Abidjan, July 1988.   123
26 American gallery-owner buying trade beads from a Hausa
   merchant in the Treichville market place. Abidjan, December
   1987.   126
27 Young Hausa trader with a display of trade beads at his market-
   place stall. Treichville quarter, Abidjan, July 1988.   127
28 Hausa trader at his stall in the front of the Plateau market place.
   Abidjan, November 1988.   134
29 Hausa trader with wooden trunk in the back section of the
   Plateau market place. Abidjan, May 1988.   135
30 Hausa trader unloading a shipment of Asante stools at Kennedy
   airport. New York, June 1989.   137
31 A carver repairing the arm on an Asante female figure. Plateau
   market place, Abidjan, January 1988.   141
32 Storehouse assistant embellishing Dan masks with padded
   cowrie-covered headdresses. Treichville quarter, Abidjan,
   November 1987.   142
33 Small Akan brass boxes stained with potassium permanganate to
   dull the surface finish. Plateau market place, Abidjan, July 1988.   143

34 Dan wooden face masks covered with kola nut compound to
    imitate the surface texture of a mask that had received
    "traditional "sacrifices. Man, June 1988.   144
35 Asante combs splattered with a kola nut residue. Plateau
    market place, Abidjan, March 1988.   145
36 Baule figure with beaded waistband and necklace. Reproduced
    by permission of the Peabody Museum, Harvard University.
    Photograph by Hillel Burger.   146
37 Baule figure with cotton loin-cloth affixed around its waist.
    Reproduced by permission of the Musée de l'Homme, Paris.
    Photograph by Charles Lemzaouda.   147
38 Baule figure showing partially removed wooden "loin-cloth."
    Private collection. Photograph by Hillel Burger.   149
39 Baule "colonial" figure wearing Western-style cap, shirt,
    shorts, sandals, and wristwatch. Private collection. Photograph
    by C. B. Steiner.   150
40 Guinean workshop artist with "colonial" figures. Port de
    Carena, Abidjan, June 1988.   151
41 Workshop apprentice painting "colonial" figures. Bouaké,
    December 1988.   152
42 Dioula trader sanding down the paint from a lot of newly arrived
    "colonial" figures. Plateau market place, Abidjan, June 1988.   153

Unless indicated otherwise, all photographs are by the author.

Acknowledgments

The research for this book was undertaken in several phases: a preliminary trip to Côte d'Ivoire in the summer of 1986 funded by a travel grant from the Department of Anthropology at Harvard University; an extended period of field research from October 1987 to October 1988 funded jointly by a Fulbright Fellowship from the Institute of International Education and a Sinclair Kennedy Travelling Fellowship from Harvard; a return visit in the summer of 1991; and a short period of library and museum research in France during the summer of 1992 funded by the American Council of Learned Societies. The original dissertation upon which this book is based was rewritten for publication from 1990–91 under the auspices of a Kalbfleisch Postdoctoral Fellowship at the American Museum of Natural History in New York. The Natural History Museum of Los Angeles County provided a conducive environment from which to make the final revisions to the manuscript. It is with great pleasure that I acknowledge all of the institutions and funding agencies that have helped to make this book better or, indeed, even possible.

I wish to thank the government of the République de Côte d'Ivoire for permitting me to conduct my field research. My affiliation in 1987–88 with the Université Nationale de Côte d'Ivoire was granted by Touré Bakary. Joachim Bony authorized and oversaw my position as Research Associate at the Institut d'Histoire, d'Art et d'Archéologie Africain in Abidjan. A. D. Hauhouot Asseypo and The Honorable J. J. Bechio wrote letters of introduction that were worth their weight in gold. I thank them all for their assistance and for the seriousness with which they took my project.

During my years of training at Harvard, I benefited immensely from the example of Sally Falk Moore, who provided generous advice and offered critical insight into the theoretical possibilities of my work. Her friendship and guidance have motivated me throughout the course of my studies and the beginning of my career. Jane Guyer, Charles Lindholm, David Maybury-Lewis, Pauline Peters, Parker Shipton, Stanley Tambiah, and Nur Yalman have helped me situate my research within the broader context of anthropological history and thought. I have profited tremendously from listening to them all. Monni Adams has shared with enthusiasm her extensive knowledge of West

African art and culture. Her stream of constructive commentary on my work has been indispensable. I owe thanks to Kalman Applbaum, Paul Brodwin, Bart Dean, Paul Gelles, Richard Grinker, Bapa Jhala, Ingrid Jordt, Mike Lambert, Jay Levi, Terry O'Nell, Norbert Peabody, and Anna Simons – who were always there at the right time. Without their camaraderie, the early stages of writing this book would have been a much lonelier task.

Preliminary bibliographic research was undertaken at the National Museum of African Art, Smithsonian Institution, where Janet Stanley offered invaluable assistance. My work at Harvard was immeasurably aided by the exceptional collections and knowledgeable staff at the Tozzer and Widener Libraries, as well as at the Peabody Museum. The Musée de l'Homme and Bibliothèque Nationale in Paris provided generous access to their collections. The American Cultural Center in Abidjan administered the Fulbright Fellowship, and contributed logistical support. While in Abidjan, Christopher Fitzgerald, George Hegarty, Nancy Nolan, Stephan Ruiz, Ray Silverman, and Ellen Suthers offered some much-needed motivation and direction at difficult junctures in the research.

My formative thoughts on the subjects of transcultural trade, the anthropology of art, and the political economy of taste were developed as an undergraduate at The Johns Hopkins University. For their help in forming my initial ideas, and for their sustaining interest in my work, I am indebted particularly to David William Cohen, Richard Price, and Sally Price, as well as to Philip Curtin, Sidney Mintz, John Murra, William Sturtevant, and Katherine Verdery. My specific ideas about the research and writing of this book were refined and improved upon through my conversations with Paula Ben-Amos, Gillian Feeley-Harnick, Christraud Geary, Stephen Gudeman, Margaret Hardin, Jean Hay, Ivan Karp, Bennetta Jules-Rosette, Sidney Kasfir, Simon Ottenberg, Philip Ravenhill, Enid Schildkrout, Susan Vogel, Richard Werbner, and Savané Yaya. Revisions to the final draft benefited from a careful reading by Michael Herzfeld, and from the suggestions made by the anonymous reviewers chosen by the press. Some of the direct quotations from African art traders that appear in the book were recorded on video in the course of my collaboration with Ilisa Barbash and Lucien Taylor on the making of *In and Out of Africa*, an ethnographic documentary about the trade in African art distributed by the University of California Extension Center for Media and Independent Learning, 2176 Shattuck Ave., Berkeley, CA 94704.

All the maps in this book were expertly drawn by Lee Nathaniel Saffel, who somehow managed to transform my sloppy sketch of an Abidjan market place into a professional illustration. My color field photographs were printed in black-and-white by John De Leon, Richard Meier, and Donald Meyer. I am grateful for all of their hard work.

To my parents, Nancy and Erwin Steiner, I owe special thanks for their unflagging encouragement, their generous support, and their persistence in trying to understand what it is I actually study. To Kathy Skelly, I am grateful for the clarity of her editorial assistance and for the inspiration she has provided throughout the course of researching and writing this book.

Finally, to those who contributed most centrally to this book, I owe the art traders in Côte d'Ivoire a tremendous debt of gratitude which I can never repay – the kind of debt with which many of them are unfortunately all too familiar. The traders welcomed me into the fold of their professional brotherhood, allowed me to observe the inner workings of their business, extended their hospitality and trust, and unselfishly shared with me the vast riches of their knowledge. Without their collaboration this book could never have been realized.

Introduction
The anthropology of African art in a transnational market

In the first decades of this century, the discipline of social anthropology defined its subject matter as the study of the inner workings of closed social systems which were isolated supposedly both from the external world and from one another. The choice for this unit of study was developed in part as a reaction against the conjectures of cultural diffusionism – a then current theory which stressed how cultural traits and material culture diffused around the world. Rather than look at the movement of peoples and things from one socio-economic context to the next, social anthropology – whose theories were to become grounded in its methods of localized and intensive ethnographic field-work – claimed as its focus of analysis the single tribe, the isolated community, and the remote village. "[E]ach society with its characteristic culture," writes Eric Wolf, "[was] conceived as an integrated and bounded system, set off against other equally bounded systems" (1982: 4).

In the past twenty-five years or so, anthropology has reacted strongly against the fiction of "primitive" isolates – deconstructing the internal architecture of putatively autonomous and self-regulating systems. The critique has taken essentially two paths. First, at the local level, the definition of the "system" itself has been revised to include "process" (i.e., history, competition, and social change). Key words associated with the earlier model of society – homeostasis, cohesion, and balance – have been replaced by new concepts such as pluralism, heterogeneity, crisis, conflict, and transformation. Second, at the supra-local level, the model of "bounded systems" has been challenged by those who see the world itself as a transformative force defined by historical processes and, in particular, shaped by the conflicts and contradictions of a capitalist world economy. In this formulation, the vision of the world has returned, in a curious fashion, to one espoused by the early diffusionists – that is to say, the world as global matrix, with transnational contacts and macro-scale linkages.[1]

Drawing inspiration both from Immanuel Wallerstein's research on the sociology of the modern world system (1974, 1979) and from Fernand Braudel's research on the social history of global commerce (1973, 1982), anthropologists engaged in the formulation of this second revisionist model have been turning their attention increasingly to the migration of persons and things in the transnational world economy. Expanding the focal range in the ethnographic lens, the subject of social anthropology has been pushed beyond the conventional community setting. Attention to global interdependence and cross-cultural exchange has revealed, as George Marcus and Michael Fischer have recently stated, an array of political and economic processes which "are registered in the activities of dispersed groups or individuals whose actions have mutual, often unintended, consequences for each other, as they are connected by markets and other major institutions that make the world a system" (1986: 91).

One way of constructing a "multilocale" ethnography within the boundaries of a single text is to trace the movement of particular commodities through space and time. Sidney Mintz, in *Sweetness and Power* (1985), tracks the history of sugar as a vehicle for analyzing the development of Afro-Caribbean slavery, the rise of Western capitalism, and the emergence of a transatlantic diaspora of mercantile accumulation. Eric Wolf, in *Europe and the People Without History* (1982), deals with the mobility of several commodities – reconstructing the major political and economic patterns of world history in order to shed light on the relationship among far-separated populations whose lives were entangled in a swirl of transglobal trade. And in *The Social Life of Things* (1986), a volume of collected essays edited by Arjun Appadurai, the contributors follow the circulation of objects (or groups of objects) as they move through specific cultural and historical milieus. Because a commodity does not always stay in the context for which it was intended, nor does it necessarily remain in the region within which it was produced, a commodity is said to have a "social life," whose value, spirit, and meaning changes through time.

This book is about the trade in African art in Côte d'Ivoire, West Africa (Map 1).[2] It is about the circulation of art objects through local, national, and transnational economies, and it is about those whose lives are caught up in its supply, distribution, and exchange. The book takes as its unit of study a group of both itinerant and settled merchants who specialize in the commerce of African art – middlemen who link either village-level object-owners, or contemporary artists and artisans, to Western collectors, dealers, and tourists. The "community" of traders is made up of members from many different ethnic groups, and represents individuals from a whole range of social back-grounds and from various levels of economic success. Because the merchandise that the traders buy and sell is defined, classified, and evaluated largely in terms of Western concepts such as "art" and "authenticity," the traders are not only moving a set of objects through the world economic system, they are also exchanging information – mediating, modifying, and commenting on a broad spectrum of cultural knowledge.

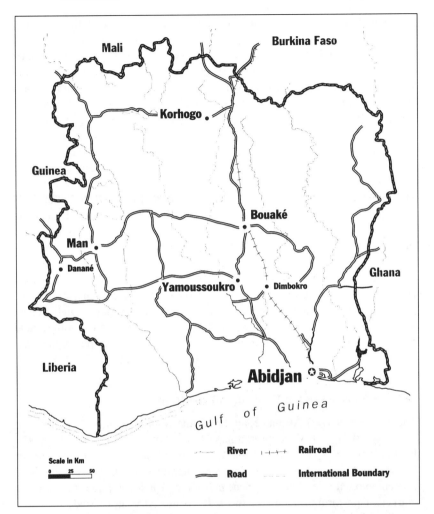

Map 1 Côte d'Ivoire.

Much of the fieldwork for this study was carried out in the market places of Abidjan – principally among art traders of Hausa, Mande, and Wolof ethnicity. Research was also undertaken in the markets of Yamoussoukro, Bouaké, Korhogo, and Man, as well as in several rural supply entrepôts including Danané in the west and Dimbokro in central Côte d'Ivoire. In addition, I spent part of my time in the field traveling through various districts of the country with Abidjan-based traders who purchase art from rural middlemen. Such travel was done both by public transportation and in a vehicle which I purchased at the beginning of the fieldwork. Documentary research in Côte d'Ivoire was undertaken in the Archives Nationales, the Université Nationale de Côte d'Ivoire, the Office National du Tourisme, and the Centre de Documentation at the Ministère de la Culture et de l'Information. Interviews were also conducted with Abidjan-based European and American dealers and collectors. The research was conducted largely in French (the language of intermediacy in the market place). A basic knowledge of Dioula helped, however, to gain access to rural traders.[3] Interviews in the market place were mostly conducted without a tape recorder.[4] The names of the traders which appear in the book have been changed in order to protect their identity. All conversions from local Ivoirian currency to American currency are based on an average exchange rate for 1987–88 of 300 CFA francs to one US dollar. Field data are referenced according to the date in which they were recorded in my notes, and dates are American style, i.e. month, day, year.

A history of the West African art trade

The art trade in West Africa began during the colonial period in the first two decades of the twentieth century. Since its inception, the principal entrepôts of international trade (in francophone West Africa) have been in the cities of Dakar and Abidjan – both of which were important administrative centers of French colonial rule. Although Senegalese merchants controlled much of the market in its formative period, the bulk of the African art trade has been distributed since the late 1950s among three major ethnic groups: Wolof of Senegal, Hausa of Niger and Nigeria, and Mande of Mali, Burkina Faso, Guinea, and Côte d'Ivoire. All of these ethnic groups have historical links to the spread of mercantile capitalism in West Africa and, in particular, all of them have been responsible for the formation of cross-cultural trading diasporas throughout the region.

Two developments, which occurred at roughly the same time but in different parts of the world, are in large measure responsible for the formation of the art trade in West Africa. The first development was the "discovery" of African art at the turn of the century by European artists and intellectuals, such as Matisse, Picasso, Braque, Vlaminck, and Apollinaire. Their interest in

African forms and aesthetics stimulated a slowly rising demand for African art objects in Europe. At first, the demand was limited largely to the Cubists and their immediate entourage. But by the 1910–20s, the demand for African art in Europe had already spread to other sectors of the society. In particular, the end of the First World War brought about an atmosphere in France which was conducive to engaging the interest of a wider public in the appreciation and collection of African art (cf. W. Cohen 1980: 284–85). The disdain in which Africans had previously been held by the great majority of France's population was replaced after the war "by a certain curiosity about the customs of these [African] people who had fought fiercely [against the Germans] and were now joyful partners in the victory celebrations" (Paudrat 1984: 157). The success of the African pavilion at the Exposition Coloniale de Vincennes in 1931 fueled even further the demand for African objects in France (Laude 1971: 20). Even after the Cubist movement had ended, and many of the artists themselves had lost all interest in African art, the *market* for African art, which they had inspired and helped organize, had already developed its own commercial structure and economic force – enabling it to continue and flourish without their support.[5]

While interest in African art was slowly emerging in Europe – spreading further and further outside the inner circle of modern primitivists – European presence in Africa was growing at a curious pace, as the scramble for the continent unfolded. By the 1920s, after most parts of West Africa had been conquered by and divided among the major European powers, colonial administrations were set into place, thereby securing commercial access to West Africa by metropole-based trading companies and expatriate firms.[6] The colonial administration in Afrique Occidentale Française (AOF) granted special rights and privileges to some of their most "loyal" subjects. The Senegalese, in particular, who among other things were associated with the *tirailleurs sénégalais* (i.e., a group of armed forces who fought for France to conquer vast territories of West Africa) were protected by colonial rule and granted access to virtually all the territories in West Africa which were administered by the French (Manning 1988: 63–64).

This new form of transnational socio-political hierarchy, which emerged during the colonial period in West Africa, allowed for members of certain ethnic groups (such as the Wolof of Senegal) to displace themselves with increased security and greater facility (Challenor 1979; Echenberg 1991). Under protection of European colonial rule, these groups were able to travel across what had once been hostile and dangerous geo-political and ethnic frontiers. Increased access for commercial pursuits by both European and African entrepreneurs meant not only that Europeans had found new potential markets for the sale of their goods in the colonies (Steiner 1985), but it meant also that the colonies had found a new source of demand for their goods in

Europe. Although most of the exports which were made by colonial trading firms were of raw materials forged on the back of cheap labor, somewhere in the shadows of these vast commercial ventures one finds the small, tentative beginnings of an African art trade.

The career of one of the first professional African art dealers in Europe, Paul Guillaume, was launched accidentally by a curious intersection of these two historical developments.[7] Guillaume's initial interest in African art was sparked in 1911 by the unanticipated visit of artist Joseph Brummer. "Informed by Apollinaire of the presence of an African object of quality in the window of an automobile appliance store," writes Jean-Louis Paudrat, "Brummer negotiated its purchase from the young clerk [Guillaume] and induced him to show him regularly the 'fetishes' received by the clerk's firm through its colonial rubber supplies" (Paudrat 1984: 152; cf. Donne 1978: 107). Within a year of Brummer's visit, Guillaume had quit his job at the automobile supply shop, and had begun actively to seek his own supply of African art. From 1912 to 1920, Guillaume continuously increased his shipments of art from rubber contractors in West Africa, and began to place advertisements in the colonial press for the purpose of extending the range of his stock (Paudrat 1984: 153). By the 1920s, Guillaume had opened his first gallery on rue La Boétie in Paris. He continued to search for new suppliers of African art by developing a network of contacts with colonial officials from AOF. At Le Bréhant, a Parisian café frequented by officials on leave from the colonies, Guillaume posted a sign which read: "Paul Guillaume pays high prices for all pieces and collections of African origin" (Paudrat 1984: 160).[8]

Although the historical record is decidedly silent about the role of the African middleman in supplying colonial agents with the artworks which were being exported to the metropole, it would not be imprudent to infer that the commercial exporters who were shipping African objects to European dealers, such as Paul Guillaume (as well as Carl Einstein, Charles Vignier, Pierre Verité, Charles Ratton, and others), were not collecting the art themselves from the remote rural villages from which the objects were being extracted. As in so many other modes of extraction which, at different moments in the African past, have supplied a variety of export commodities for shipment to the West – the most obvious case being the Atlantic slave trade – it was the African intermediary who provided the first and most vital link in the commercial chain.

From the 1920–30s onward, the trade in African art became increasingly structured and organized on the side of supply. By this time, African artists had already started reproducing objects expressly for the export market. Some of these pieces were being commissioned by local colonial administrators, either for their own collections or as gifts for their friends and family in the metropole. Others were already being marketed from stalls and storehouses owned by African traders in French colonial capitals, such as Dakar and Abidjan. By the 1950s, African art traders from AOF were regularly making the journey to France to sell objects directly to European-based dealers.[9] As the supply diminished of what the Western collector defines as the "classic" genres of African art – ideally, wooden face masks and ritual statuary (see Rubin 1984: 15–17) – traders expanded their inventory to include other categories of "art," such as household or utilitarian items, furniture, textiles, etc.

From very early on in the trade, newly carved objects were being artificially aged – their patina, coloration, and surface wear being carefully altered – so that the objects could be marketed in the West as antique or "authentic" art. During the decades of the 1960–70s, the art market in West Africa had probably reached its boom. Not only had an extensive demand been created in Europe, but also by this time demand had reached the shores of America. "The Peace Corps, the civil-rights movement, African nationalism, and the beginning of mass tourism to West Africa," writes Nicholas Lemann, "all increased American interest in African art" (1987: 26). In the late 1970s, most analysts would probably agree, the art market in West Africa had started to take a downward turn. Economic recessions in the West and diminishing supplies in Africa both contributed to a sluggish market and a deflationary spiral. While the market for the resale of African art from private collections was ignited by the economic bonfire of the 1980s – with record prices being set at one auction after another – the West African side of the trade smoldered, never returning to where it had been during the 1960–70s. Part of the reason for this is that many buyers had become convinced that all examples of "genuine" African art had already been taken out of the continent. The economic competition in the African art market had thus shifted from the site of original supply in Africa to the locus of the recirculation of previously owned objects in the West. While the market, in Côte d'Ivoire alone, still currently supports several hundred full-time African traders and middlemen, its scale has been significantly reduced by the combined negative forces of diminishing supply and dwindling demand. Although new traders keep entering the market each year, their economic returns keep going down and their future grows increasingly uncertain.

African art through the lens of commerce

The study of African art has tended to concentrate on the function or aesthetics of various forms of art within the context of a single, highly localized ethnographic setting.[10] In order to describe a given art form in what is supposedly its most pristine or "authentic" state, scholars specializing in the study of African art have often isolated the unit of analysis without taking into account the effects of outside influence.[11] Such a mode of investigation is inevitably artificial since it is arguable that at no time has African art existed in total cultural isolation. In recent years, studies of African art have begun to take more seriously the impact of outside forces on local artistic expression. Some recent works, for example, have taken into account: (1) the complexity of ethnic attribution in African arts (e.g., the movement of objects for ritual use across ethnic boundaries); (2) the impact of the world economic system on local artistic production (e.g., the manufacturing of so-called "tourist" or "airport" arts); (3) the articulation of Islam and other world religions with indigenous African beliefs in the creation of syncretic sacred arts; and (4) the incorporation of Western manufactured products (plastic dolls, factory-made cloth, industrial hardware, etc.) into so-called "traditional" contexts.

Although the field of vision has widened greatly in the past few years, one area of research which remains largely unexplored is the commercial aspect of African art and, in particular, the analysis of the specialized trading diasporas which are used to circulate art objects throughout the African continent and the rest of the world. There are several reasons, I believe, which account for the lack of interest among scholars in the African art trade. First, like the study of markets in general, the study of art markets may appear initially to be a daunting task – requiring the understanding of a complex system characterized by extensive verbal bargaining, complicated credit relations, and a nearly untraceable network of circulating goods and capital. The study of the African art trade by a *Westerner* is made even more problematic by the very fact that the investigator belongs by definition to the consumer class and, as a result, is often considered to be a potential buyer of art rather than simply a patron of ideas.[12]

Second, the study of the African art market poses many of the same problems as the study of an African secret society – with the added obstacle that most traders do not want the investigator to become an initiate. Trade secrets cover a broad spectrum of activities. Traders, for example, are reluctant to talk about their earnings (for fear that kin, friends, or other traders will want to borrow money); they will not speak readily of their commercial success (almost all traders returning to Africa from Europe or America will try to discourage others from going abroad by saying that business is generally bad); they will not display or reveal their entire stock (for they know that the fewer times an object is seen, the higher its potential value will remain);[13] they will not easily reveal either the sources of their goods or their network of clients (for one of the key functions of traders is to maintain their status as middlemen, by keeping apart both village object-owners and producers from Western consumers); and, lastly, they will not divulge freely their techniques of artificial aging or mechanical patination (so as, understandably, to keep the buyers somewhat mystified).

Third, because the study of African art has developed largely in conjunction with the collection of African art in the West, I would argue that those who study African art (especially those trained as art historians) have been disinclined to write about a system which makes of aesthetic objects temporary commodities in the "middle passage" from African village to Western vitrine. In the collection of African art by Westerners, the aesthetic value of an object is usually given more overt attention than its economic value.[14] Moreover, since the collection of African art is often associated with an idealized Western vision of static "primitive" culture, most collectors, I believe, would prefer to read about the uses of African art in a putatively unchanging pre-colonial milieu than about the commoditization of African art in a post-colonial trans-national economy.[15]

Finally, there has been a tendency among Western scholars and collectors alike to dismiss African art traders as "misinformed" or "ignorant," and unable, therefore, to truly appreciate or recognize the aesthetic merit and ethnographic provenance of what they sell.[16] Traders are often treated by Westerners with disrespect, and sometimes even with unbecoming disdain. Most of the traders who travel with their merchandise to Europe and America are described by Westerners as "runners," while their Western counterparts who travel to Africa to purchase large volumes of art for export to the West are referred to by the far more genteel and prestigious term "dealers." The implication of this semantic discrimination, I would argue, is closely related to a distinction which is commonly drawn between the African artist and the Western connoisseur. While the latter is said to be capable of judging aesthetic qualities and of ranking the relative "importance" of different works of African art, the former, it is said, simply produces his work spontaneously – oblivious somehow to the "genius" which guides his own hand (Price 1989: 87–89). The African art trader, in a similar tone, is often described as one who handles "masterpieces" without knowledge or care; he is portrayed as a blind supplier of raw materials (hence the word "runner") whose goods are "transformed" by the Western dealer who, contrary to his African counterpart, is entirely capable of appreciating what he sells (cf. Taylor and Brooke 1969). When collectors of African art buy from Western dealers, they expect to be guided by the seller's good taste and judgment. In general, they neither expect to be cheated by the dealer, nor to cheat the dealer themselves. When these same individuals buy the same sort of objects from an African "runner," they expect only to encounter deceit – either to be misguided by the seller into buying a "fake," or, conversely, to misguide the seller by buying something from him which is actually worth far more than the price at which he agrees to sell. As Lemann puts it, those who "patronize the runners [are] convinced that these people – usually illiterate and speaking only broken English – can't possibly know what the stuff they're selling is really worth" (1987: 28). The wife of a collector in New York told me once that her husband saw nearly every African "runner" that called him at his

Manhattan office. "He keeps hoping to find that one masterpiece, like a real Fang reliquary figure or something, buried somewhere in the junk that the runners usually sell" (12/20/89).

Hence, on the one hand, the economic quality of a trader's merchandise is ignored in order to draw attention away from the monetary value of the category "art." And, on the other hand, the artistic/cultural elements which make up the trader's craft are dismissed since it is believed that only the Western buyer or dealer is really capable of appreciating aesthetic worth. For all the reasons listed above, then, the African art trader has been relegated by silence to an invisible cog in the wheels of a complex transnational market – a market which functions because of, *not* in spite of, the African middleman.

Analysis of the African art trade not only sheds light on a "forgotten" people, it also illuminates an important facet of African art which has generally been neglected in the literature. By broadening the parameters of discernible influence, the study of the art trade integrates areas hitherto treated in relative isolation. Because traders move continually back-and-forth from local to global economy, a study of the art market sheds light on the impact of Western consumption on African art and aesthetics. Exogenous demand has not only encouraged traders to drain villages of their artistic wealth, but it has also led to the creation of new forms of material culture (hybrid styles, invented genres, replicas, and fakes) constructed, in James Clifford's apposite phrase, from the "debris of colonial culture contact" (1985: 166). Hence, the study of the African art trade uncovers not only a complex economic system with its own internal structure, logic, and rules, it reveals also an elaborate process of cross-cultural exchange in which the image of Africa and its arts are continually being negotiated and redefined by a plurality of market participants spread out across the world.

Paradigms in the study of African art

This book draws upon and contributes to several different bodies of literature, including those on the sociology of the market place, the linguistics of verbal bargaining, the structuring of ethnicity in cross-cultural trade, the political economy of commoditization, and the dynamics of cultural brokerage or the mediation of knowledge. Most components of these diverse bodies of literature are referenced and discussed in the places of the book where they are most relevant. In this section, therefore, I have chosen to restrict my discussion to the literature on African art, and, in particular, to locate this work within the history of scholarship on African art and material culture.

The study of African art developed largely in conjunction with the discipline of anthropology at the beginning of this century. Some of the earliest works on African art were written in order to further particular claims within a broader debate between diffusionist and evolutionist schools of thought. African art was used either as visual evidence for the spread of cultural traits from innovative centers to imitative peripheries, or as evidence for the social evolution of cultures – from groups which were supposedly capable of only naturalistic representation to those which had presumably graduated to the mastery of geometric stylization and abstract forms (Silver 1979a: 270–71; Gerbrands 1990: 15–17).

As the field of anthropology altered its emphasis from diffusion to context, and from evolution to function, the study of African art followed in its path. Drawing upon the new discourse of anthropology, and in particular taking a lead from Malinowski and Radcliffe-Brown, the focus in the study of African art was to become the indigenous context – which would reveal the place of art within a balanced holistic system of social and cultural functions. In this sense, art was understood simply as yet another vital organ in the proper maintenance and functioning of a stable social organism. Eventually, the term "ethno-aesthetics" came to be used as a label for this type of approach. Faced with an abundance of non-Western art in the repositories of Western museums, ethno-aesthetics was conceived as an analytic method to resituate these objects within the environment of their original use. Philip Dark wrote in 1967:

At this time, when so many art forms from non-western cultures are being sold in our cities in increasing numbers, one might say en-masse, while the buyers remain, to a large extent, ignorant of the context in which they were made, we have need of anthropologists who can help bring understanding of art in context to those who have some of its results *hors de contexte*. (1967: 133)

By the early 1970s, anthropologists had begun to question the privileged place of "context" within the study and analysis of African art. Increasingly aware of the permeability of the boundaries which surrounded the area of study, scholars began to peer through some of the cracks in the imagined borders which putatively encased the art in its indigenous milieu. "There is no *a priori* guarantee that a particular linguistic or other group or sub-group identified in advance by the researcher, no matter how ingeniously characterized," wrote Whitney Davis recently, "is, in fact, the full and real context of and for a particular history of representations" (1989: 26).

In challenging what was perceived to be an overemphasis on local context, research on African art took two directions. First, the local context itself was broadened and redefined to include inter-group relations and contacts. In so doing, it was discovered that art objects were not only created for local use, but were also borrowed and traded among ethnic groups within a wide geographic terrain – both art and artists moving from place to place, crosscutting and penetrating an array of so-called ethnic "boundaries" (Bravmann 1973; Frank 1987). "Interaction, not isolation," summarizes Monica Visonà, "seems to characterize much of the production and distribution of traditional art forms. Yet African art is still presented to the general public as if there were a representative style for each ethnic group and as if each piece were either a typical or atypical example of a single population's oeuvre" (1987: 38).

Second, the unit of analysis was expanded not only to include contacts within and among a wide range of proximate ethnic groups, but also to include the impact of international tourism on local art production. This literature, which is gathered generally under the heading of "tourist art" studies, has tended to be of two sorts. On the one hand, there have been works which have described and analyzed the production and manufacture of art objects for sale to tourists (e.g., see Ben-Amos 1971, 1976; Silver 1976, 1979b, 1981a, 1981b; Richter 1980; Ross and Reichert 1983; Wolff 1985). These studies have dealt with such issues as the social relations of production in communities of petty craft manufacturers, the organization of apprenticeship and the incorporation of workers in a local artisanal economy, and the impact of new artistic forms on the social system of artistic production. The focus has been primarily on the local level. How have artists and artisan groups reacted or adapted to outside demand? How have styles of art been changed or modified for foreign consumption? How has production for internal use been articulated with production for external use?

On the other hand, there have been a number of works which have attempted to place tourist art within the semiotic domain of a system of signs. Using a linguistic model, these studies have analyzed tourist art as a "process of communication involving image creators who attempt to represent aspects of their own cultures to meet the expectations of image consumers who treat art as an example of the exotic" (Jules-Rosette 1984: 1). One of the earliest and most conceptually imaginative studies of this genre is Paula Ben-Amos's seminal paper on "Pidgin Languages and Tourist Arts" (1977), in which tourist arts are compared to secondary trade languages and analyzed as a special-purpose, restricted, and standardized code used expressly for cross-cultural communication. Whether they are examining the production of objects or the production of meanings, the level of analysis in both types of tourist art studies has tended to be the local artistic community – i.e., restricting themselves to the production end in a transnational market of cross-cultural exchange.

In the past few years, the study of African tourist art production has been complemented by a series of works on the consumption of African art (or, more usually, of "primitive" art in general) in the West (e.g., Clifford 1985, 1988; Jamin 1982, 1985; Manning 1985; MacClancy 1988; Errington 1989; Price 1989; Torgovnick 1990). These works have sought to unpack the symbolic load with which African art objects are charged when they are displayed out of context. Rather than use the study of decontextualized objects as a stepping stone to an analysis which seeks to resituate the objects in their "indigenous" context, the displacement of the object itself is taken as the problematic and focus of research. Reflecting upon the very same collections of non-Western art that prompted a previous generation of anthropologists to want to know more about the meaning of these objects in the places from which they came, some anthropologists are now wondering how these objects came to be wrenched from the places in which they were made and what they mean now in the places where they have come to rest. Studies of this sort pose some of the following type of questions. Why have these objects been moved to where they are? What are the political and economic forces which have allowed cultural property to be removed from their original owners? And what do they mean now that they are situated in this new milieu?

Because the symbols of African art are silent outside their original community of spokespersons, the objects are themselves tabula rasa – virgin icons upon which observers imprint their own significance and interpretation. "Stripped of its original authorship and, more generally, of conceptual footnotes," writes Sally Price, "the object stands nakedly before the gaze of the Western viewer" (1989: 106). And, writing in a similar language, Georges Balandier once remarked, "objects under glass [are] as helpless in the presence of sightseers as the dead in the presence of the crowds on All Saints' Day. Both are 'defenseless', so that we have unlimited freedom to consider and treat them as we please" (1967: 100). Symbols that make no reference to sexuality in their original context are charged by the Western viewer with raw sexual connotations. Portraits of living spirits are mistaken for representations of the dead or, more generally, they are glossed as idols in a cult of ancestor worship. Emblems of beauty and peace are misinterpreted as signs of fear and terror.

By studying the mechanisms of exchange which move art objects from Africa to the rest of the world, this book bridges the distance between the field of production and the field of consumption. It provides, so to say, the "missing link(s)" in a long commercial chain which stretches from the smallest rural villages in West Africa to the largest urban centers in the Western world.[17] In particular, the study of the exchange of African art throws light on two distinct processes which occur at the intermediate level of the art market. First, the study documents the process of commoditization. It explores the way in which objects are moved from one system of value to another, and describes the mechanisms by which values are assigned to objects at each stage in the network of trade. In so doing, it analyzes a distinct moment in the "life history" of African art – i.e., a commodity phase which separates an object both from its "traditional" sphere of value as ritual or sacred icon, and its "modernist" sphere of value as *objet d'art*. Second, it illustrates an elaborate process of cross-cultural information exchange or, what I will refer to more generally as, the mediation of knowledge. The study suggests that in their commercial pursuits art traders are not mindlessly moving goods from one place to another, they are also mediating between art producers and art consumers – adding economic value to what they sell by interpreting and capitalizing on the cultural values and desires from two different worlds. This book, therefore, is as much about the *transit* of African objects in the commercial space of the modern world system as it is about the *transition* of African objects at a distinct moment and critical time in the history of Africa and its arts.

The book is divided into six chapters. Approximately the first half of the book is devoted to a study of the economic structure of the trade. The second half is largely about the trade in cultural information and the mediation of knowledge. In Chapter 1, I describe the basic structure of the Ivoirian art market – providing a description of the different commodity outlets and a classification of the type of goods that are sold at different levels of the trade. In Chapter 2, I describe the division of labor in the market and examine the management of capital, in particular the systems of credit and commission payments both within the market place and a trader's personal network of clients.

In Chapter 3, I analyze the production of value in the market economy, and present an analysis of four different modes of bargaining or verbal price negotiation. It is demonstrated, in this chapter, that each level in the bargaining process is associated with a different structuring of value. The bargaining process, it is suggested, is aimed largely at gauging the worth of an object in the transactor's value system.

Chapter 4 opens with an extended case study recounting an episode during my fieldwork in which an art trader from one ethnic group cut across the market hierarchy to buy directly from a supplier from a different ethnic group. The conflict which ensues from his action is described in detail and then analyzed in order to throw light on the nature of ethnic relations within the market context. The chapter goes on to look more broadly at the role of ethnicity in the art market – from a discussion of cross-cultural trade to an analysis of the commoditization of ethnicity itself.

In Chapter 5, I discuss the concept of authenticity as it applies to the art market. It begins with an overview of some of the definitions of authenticity in African art which are most widely held both by Western scholars and art collectors. It then goes on to examine the notion of authenticity from the perspective of the African art traders. Analysis of two cases – one on the commoditization of slingshots, and the other on the symbolic transformation of trade beads – serves to illustrate some of the points that are made at the beginning of the chapter. It is argued throughout that the authenticity of African art is a Western construction that is based on powerful economic and culturally hegemonic motives.

In Chapter 6, I bring together much of the preceding material by analyzing the role of art traders as cultural brokers or mediators of knowledge. While traders relate to artists some of the preferences and desires of the Western clientele, they also communicate to the clientele a particular image of African art and culture. I demonstrate in this chapter the means by which art traders manipulate both the meaning and value of objects through contextualized presentation, verbal description, and physical alteration.

Finally, in the conclusion, I present the material from the book in light of competing discourses on value. Drawing especially on Pierre Bourdieu's sociological analysis of the "mis-recognition" of cultural capital, I demonstrate how the Western (e)valuation of African art builds itself in direct opposition to both use value and exchange value.

1 Commodity outlets and the classification of goods

> To walk into a market place . . . is to wonder how one can really go about studying it. The market place itself is often large and amorphous; buyers and seller look alike; the products are probably mostly unfamiliar, and the measures of quantity and the means for calculating value unusual; the process of exchange may either be so rapid as to be almost incomprehensible, or very slow, but with little to clarify the rationale of negotiation. There is a strong temptation to view much of the activity as erratic and pointless, particularly if one is unfamiliar with the premises of value which underlie local trade.
>
> Sidney W. Mintz, *Peasant Market Places and Economic Development in Latin America* (1964)

Entering any one of the large art market places[1] in Côte d'Ivoire is very much like penetrating the confused and dizzying world which Sidney Mintz once described for the market places of rural Latin America. As one walks amidst rows of carefully displayed objects of art in the crowded aisles of the market place, it seems almost unfathomable to understand the logic behind the division of space, the organization of the marketing arena, or the structure of the trade itself. Beside the scores of neatly aligned objects which fill the dense market space, one encounters dozens, or more often hundreds, of people wandering among the stalls, busily bargaining to make a deal, or simply sitting in small groups talking among themselves.

One of Abidjan's largest market places which specializes in the sale of art objects is situated in the heart of a public garden built by the French administration during the colonial era. From a central vantage point, somewhere in the middle of this large, labyrinthine market place, one can observe a virtual stream of human activity. A woman passes by carrying on her head a massive aluminum pot which drips with condensation from the iced water which it contains. A young man, wearing a brightly colored woolen cap, files through the market place carrying on his head an enamelware platter stacked to the edge with slabs of dried beef. Two boys, who normally earn their livelihood on the fringe of the Ivoirian economy as ambulant shoe-shiners, are crouched on the ground arduously polishing wooden masks with Johnson's paste wax (Plate 1). A tall, stately man wearing an elegant flowing damask robe and an

1 Young boys at Plateau market place polishing Senufo masks with paste wax. Abidjan, April 1988.

embroidered Muslim skullcap sits quietly on a wooden crate in front of a pile of statuettes, masks, brass castings, and bead necklaces. Some of the traders are scrutinizing the man's merchandise, haggling over a price, throwing objects down in disgust, walking away, coming back. A group of merchants saunter between stalls dragging in their hands burlap sacs pregnant with amorphous outlines of the wooden artifacts that are stuffed inside. Seated low to the ground on small wooden stools, a half-dozen men sit in a circle around a tin bowl filled to the rim with rice, vegetables, and steamed fish. As they eat, they discuss with passion such diverse topics as the upcoming soccer finals, the intrigues of national politics, and the troubled world economy.

Among this bustling and diverse crowd of people, one wonders, as an anthropologist, who are the art traders that are supposed to be selling in the market place? Who are the suppliers bringing goods from afar? Which of these people are merely idlers and curious bystanders? Where are the customers? Who owns which space in the market place? To whom do all these wondrous objects belong? And how, in essence, as Clifford Geertz once eloquently put it, can one ever hope to "reduce the surface tumult of the bazaar [economy] to the deep calm of social theory?" (1979: 197).

After several seemingly endless weeks of dutifully watching, wandering, and talking to people in the market place, a sense of order eventually begins to emerge. Far from the initial feeling of hopeless disorder and chaos which appeared to exist on the surface, one discovers that the market place is in fact a scrupulously structured social space in which every object has its rightful owner and in which every person has a specific status and a recognized set of social and economic roles. The principal art market place in Abidjan (known as the *marché artisanale du Plateau*), for example, is divided among traders representing six different francophone West African nations. Within these sections, stalls are individually maintained and rented from the Abidjan City Hall (*mairie*). Each trader who rents a stall has his own stock of merchandise which he buys and sells. Every day (except Sunday)[2] traders arrive in the market place around seven or eight in the morning to unpack their merchandise from locked metal trunks which are stored beneath the wooden tables at their stalls. After sipping a strong cup of "Senegalese" roasted coffee or (for the more wealthy traders) an espresso from the Café Kona, a Lebanese operated snackbar on the edge of the Plateau market place, the traders neatly align their wares according to object types on rows of vinyl-covered concrete or wooden shelves. Some objects are dusted or polished with a rag; each is placed where it had been just the day before. Every evening, as the sun begins to set around six o'clock, the traders pack their merchandise once again into their aluminum trunks. Since no paper or padding is ever used to protect the packed objects, items are occasionally damaged in the course of this daily routine.

At night, the market place and the trunks are looked after by a group of squatters, pickpockets, and prostitutes who make their home under the market's concrete canopies, cook their meals on small charcoal braziers, and sleep on the vinyl-covered shelves. Occasionally, the traders reward the men and women who "guard" the market at night by giving them small amounts of change. The traders note that none of their merchandise has ever been stolen. The thieves, they say, are too afraid of the spiritual power represented by the statues and masks. For good measure, however, most of the Muslim traders place paper or cloth packages of protective amulets inside their storage trunks and in the rafters above their stalls – charms, prepared by the *malamai*, that work to protect their merchandise from damage or theft.[3]

Commodity outlets

In Abidjan, the largest city and principal port of trade in Côte d'Ivoire,[4] there are several outlets for the sale of art. Art is sold from both open-air and indoor market places where traders display their goods on wooden or concrete shelves in covered stalls. Art is sold from warehouse-like shops, where merchants conduct their business from rooms jammed full with their stock-in-trade. Art is sold out of merchants' private homes and compounds, where objects are stored in cabinets, dresser drawers, and under beds. Art is sold from roadside stands along the route to seashore beaches and resorts, as well as on the beaches themselves by ambulant peddlers. Finally, art is sold in up-scale galleries (both independent stores and hotel gift shops), where objects are individually priced, carefully lighted, and displayed in climate controlled surroundings. The following is a synopsis of the different outlets where art is sold in Abidjan. I have chosen to describe in greatest detail the sale outlets in Abidjan (rather than some other urban center in Côte d'Ivoire), because Abidjan is the hub of the internal exchange system and provides the greatest quantity and variety of sale outlets.[5] The discussion is organized by order of relative importance in the local economy of the art trade.

Market places

Within Côte d'Ivoire there are four major art market centers (Abidjan, Bouaké, Korhogo, and Man). At Man, near the Liberian border in western Côte d'Ivoire, about half of the second floor of a two-story concrete structure is devoted to the sale of art. Mixed in among the textile, hardware, and produce vendors, a group of art traders proffer their goods from wooden tables and stacked shelves. A few of the traders also have small rooms with locking doors in which they can store and exhibit their art objects. In Bouaké, in the central part of the country, there are two venues for the sale of art. Outside the principal tourist hotel, Le Ran, there are about ten wooden stalls in which traders display their art. Within the main market place,[6] there is a section where a dozen or so art traders ply their ware (Plate 2). In this market place, the art objects are sold side-by-side with both traditional medicines and cotton fabrics. Although no art traders sell in the main commercial market place of Korhogo, in northern Côte d'Ivoire, there is an art market place of sorts which is set up outside the most popular tourist hotel, Le Mont Korhogo (Plate 3). Objects here are displayed on wooden tables which line both sides of the street outside the main entrance gate of the hotel.

In Abidjan there are three market places where art is sold to foreign and local buyers. The oldest and largest one is located in the heart of Abidjan's commercial district, known as the Plateau quarter. The second largest art market place is in an elite residential neighborhood called Cocody quarter. And the third is in an African residential neighborhood known as Treichville quarter (see Map 2).[7]

The smallest concentration of art is sold in what is one of the largest permanent market places in all of West Africa, which is located in Treichville quarter, one of several working-class residential neighborhoods in greater Abidjan. The market place as a whole caters to a local African clientele. It consists of a two-story, open frame concrete structure built around a huge central quadrangle. The building which houses the Treichville market place

2 Market-place stall. Bouaké, December 1987.

was constructed in the late 1960s by the newly independent Ivoirian government. Spices, fruits, and vegetables are sold by marketwomen in the open
courtyard (for an insightful ethnography of the marketwomen of Treichville,
see Lewis 1976).[8] Meat and fish, hardware, cooking implements, household
products, cosmetics, and jewelry are sold on the inside ground floor of the
building. Textiles, shoes, clothes, and some works of art are sold from
the second floor of the building. The stairs which lead to the second floor of the
market are lined with sellers of various crafts. Among Westerners visiting Côte
d'Ivoire, the market place is known principally for its European trade beads.
Vast quantities of glass beads are sold by a dozen or so traders who specialize
in bead commerce (see Chapter 5 for a discussion of the significance of the
bead trade). Furthermore, tourists often visit the market in order to experience
the vibrancy of an "authentic" African market place, with the bustle and
commotion which Western visitors have come to expect from such places.[9]
"After lunch," says the itinerary for a West African tour group, "sightseeing
includes the Treichville market" (Anon. 1987a). Thus, the market experience
in Treichville becomes as much of a tourist commodity as the souvenirs which
the traders sell (see Chapter 3 on marketing and bargaining as tourist
performances).[10]

The second largest art market, which was built in the 1970s by the post-
colonial Ivoirian government, is situated on the Boulevard de France in the

3 Traders at their stalls in front of Le Mont Korhogo Hotel. Korhogo, August 1988.

elite residential neighborhood of Cocody quarter. The art section of this market caters especially to a vast expatriate clientele who reside largely in this part of the city. Like the market place in Treichville, the Cocody market place is housed in a two-story concrete structure. Vegetables, fruits, and other foods are sold on the ground floor of the market. Art objects, crafts, and souvenirs are sold on the second floor. Sellers of leather sandals, handbags, and belts, as well as beaded bracelets and other jewelry, line the two front staircases which give public access to the second floor of the market. The Cocody market place differs from those in Treichville and Plateau quarters in that it contains large individual rooms which can be locked at night. Unlike the Plateau where objects must be packed and unpacked on a daily basis, and unlike the Treichville market place where goods are secured under tightly roped plastic covers, the Cocody market place provides permanent stores where goods can be easily secured and stored.[11] One of the results of this facility is that larger items (e.g., stools, chairs, oversized masks and statues) tend to be sold out of these stores in the Cocody market place.

The oldest permanent market place in Côte d'Ivoire where art is offered for sale is the Plateau market place. The market place was constructed by the French in the early 1920s at the center of an elegant public garden (*jardin public*),[12] at the intersection of two busy streets in the Plateau quarter

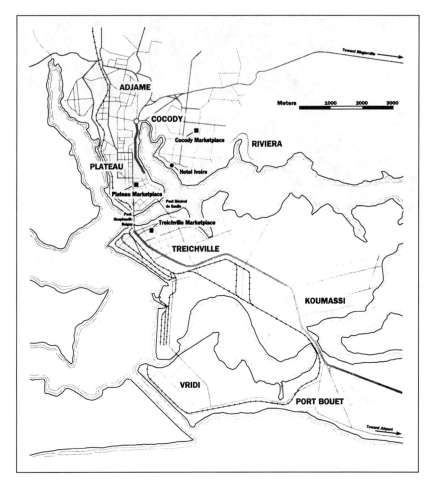

Map 2 Abidjan.

4 Partial view of the inside of an original concrete-frame stall at the Plateau
market place. The empty section in the center of the display area represents
the allotted space for a trader who did not come to the market place that day
to exhibit his merchandise. Abidjan, June 1988.

(Boulevard de la République and Avenue Chardy) and opposite the first
tourist/expatriate hotel built in Abidjan, L'Hôtel du Parc, which opened about
the same time (Nedelec 1974: 98). The Hotel du Parc shut down in the mid-
1970s.[13] Traders recall that when the hotel was in its prime during the
1940–50s, the hotel's bar, called Le Bardon (which was the hotel's original
name), was a lively place for meeting many clients and selling vast quantities
of African art. Collectors would sit on the terrace of the outdoor café across
from the market place, while traders streamed through with bags full of
art. This period, according to traders, was the heyday of the Plateau market
place.[14]

The original market place consisted of five large concrete canopies under
which traders displayed their goods on concrete ledges and shelves (Plate 4).
From about 1920 to 1970, the market was dominated largely by Wolof
merchants who had migrated from Senegal (and, for this reason, the market
place is still often referred to as the *marché sénégalais*).[15] During the 1970s,
the government of Côte d'Ivoire became concerned with the high concentration
of Senegalese traders in the art market. As part of a broader state policy to
encourage the "Ivoirianization" of the economy, the government sought to

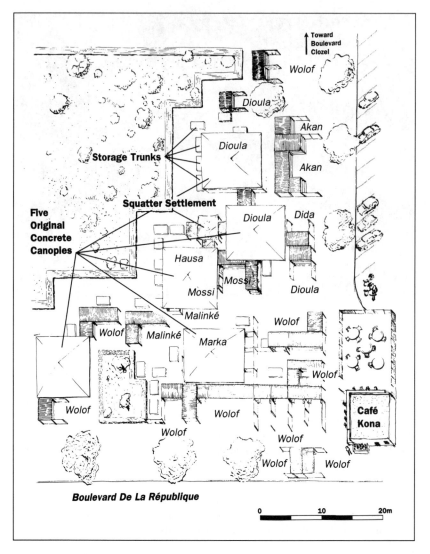

Map 3 Plan of Plateau market place, Abidjan.

5 Wooden-frame stall built in the 1970s at the Plateau market place. Abidjan,
June 1988.

break the Wolof monopoly in the art trade.[16] The Plateau market place was
officially divided among traders representing a coalition of six francophone
African nations – Côte d'Ivoire, Burkina Faso, Mali, Guinea, Niger, and
Senegal (see Map 3). Added to the original concrete canopies were wooden
frame structures with wooden display shelves covered with vinyl fabric
(Plate 5). Like many post-colonial African cities, the market place accommo-
dated its new arrivals by expanding around the rubble of a decaying colonial
structure.

The division of the market place resulted in the creation of a government-
sanctioned syndicate, the Syndicat des Antiquaires, which officially authorizes
its members to buy and sell African art in Côte d'Ivoire.[17] The syndicate is
managed largely by Ivoirian traders, however, non-Ivoirians are accepted as
members, and some hold title positions. Each member of the syndicate receives
an identification card, and pays annual dues. The syndicate is supposed to help
its members with legal problems.[18] It is also responsible for paying part of the
funeral expenses of its members.[19]

Beyond these pragmatic expectations, one of the syndicate's principal roles
is to maintain the economic viability of the middleman by restricting the
direct participation of local carvers in the sale of art to Western buyers. Hans
Himmelheber elucidates this point when he notes, "The Syndicat des

Antiquaires hinders the artists from marketing their own works. They can sell something to tourists who find them by chance, but a carver cannot travel with a bag full of masks and peddle them from a streetcorner" (1975: 25, translated from the German).[20] The state control of ethnic diversification is most strongly felt in the Plateau market place. Since the other Abidjan market places are of more recent construction (1960–70s), there was a greater degree of ethnic diversity among the traders from the very beginning.

The Plateau market place is known among collectors for selling many of the finer, more expensive pieces of African art. It is also a place where collectors can make contact with traders who will then take them to their homes or shops where even more expensive or important objects are often kept. The market place is designed in a roughly semi-circular form. Stalls along the market periphery are still run exclusively by the Wolofs who founded the market site.[21] In the center of the market place, however, stalls are divided among traders from various ethnic and national origins – including Malinké from Guinea, Hausa from Niger, Mossi and Dioula from Burkina Faso and Mali, and Baule, Guéré, and Dida from Côte d'Ivoire. A weekly fee for the usage of market space is paid by traders to the Abidjan *mairie*. The stall fee or right is collected in person by a government employee (*contrôleur*) who walks through the market place collecting money and tickets (with stall numbers printed on them) which stallholders must tear off from a booklet which they receive at the time when they rent the stall.[22] Unlike other markets, where the price of the stall right is calculated according to the type of merchandise which is being sold (Babb 1989: 104), the fee in these market places is based on the size and quality of the stall area (i.e., covered stall, open stall, fraction of a larger stall, etc.).[23]

In the early 1980s, several traders in the Plateau market place decided to expand their marketing space by selling art from wooden trunks located roughly in the center of the market. The trunks allowed these traders to divide their stock among the more commonplace tourist crafts which were displayed on shelves in the front of the market place and some of the more expensive pieces (sometimes older pieces) which were "hidden" in locked trunks. When these boxes were installed, traders say that they had enough "old" objects to fill nearly the entire trunk. Nowadays, however, they say that such objects are so hard to find that the trunk serves mainly to keep separate the good tourist copies from the poorer ones. When selling art to collectors and tourists, the location of objects in trunks makes them seem more special. Traders are very conscious of presentation; the more valuable an object is thought to be, the more layers of wrapping are used to cover it – the object is first wrapped in paper, stored in a zipped travel bag, and locked in the trunk (for more detail on the role of presentation in the marketing techniques used by traders, see Chapter 6).

6 Storehouse with proprietors. Treichville quarter, Abidjan, November 1987.

Storehouses

Hidden from the average tourist or collector in the major urban centers of Côte d'Ivoire are storehouses or warehouses in which vast quantities of objects are stockpiled (Plate 6). In Korhogo, the storehouses are located in a Hausa residential neighborhood, called Aoussabougou (see Chapter 4). In Man, there are Hausa-operated storehouses scattered in different parts of the town. In Abidjan, most of the storehouses are located in Treichville quarter. Many of these facilities are operated by Hausa traders (Plate 7).[24] Some of the storehouses face the street (with large garage-like entrances); others are built in compounds off the main street; and yet others are located in rooms within the family dwelling itself. The storehouses serve several functions. First, they are used as a kind of "dumping ground" for itinerant suppliers. Whatever a supplier is unable to sell to the market place stallholders or other local traders, he will wholesale to, or even leave on credit with, the storehouse owners. As a result of this practice, many of the storehouses are filled with piles of mediocre and inferior quality art which has been rejected by a majority of local buyers. The storehouses also serve as marketing venues for African traders who ship objects abroad, and for wholesale Western dealers who buy in Côte d'Ivoire. These buyers purchase both the low quality items which have accumulated over time, and the better quality items which are stored in smaller quantities.

Objects are packed in wooden crates or cardboard boxes, and driven directly from Treichville to the cargo docks at the international airport or to one of several shipping ports.

Another function of the art storehouses is to provide a selling space for itinerant traders. While some of the suppliers sell from the compounds they share in Abobo Gare (on the outskirts of metropolitan Abidjan), and a few sell directly in the three Abidjan market places, a number of the suppliers sell their wares out of the Treichville storehouses. One of the storehouse owners, Alhadji Salka, for instance, lent out his space to Jibrim Taroare, a Hausa supplier based in the town of Bobo-Dioulasso in Burkina Faso. Taroare would visit Abidjan roughly every six weeks. He would store his bags and boxes of objects in Salka's storehouse, and would sell to local traders from this space. Salka was given a commission based on Taroare's profits. Since Salka was elderly and partially disabled, the "rental" of his storehouse provided him with one of his few sources of regular income.[25]

Galleries

There are several art galleries in Abidjan and other urban centers which cater both to foreign African art collectors and souvenir buyers. At Yamoussoukro, there is a small gallery in the main tourist hotel, Le President. And at Man, there is a "gallery" built outside Hotel Les Cascades (Plate 8). Most of the galleries, however, that are designed according to Western criteria (i.e., with posted price tags and boutique lighting) are located in or around the major tourist hotels in Abidjan – Hotel Ivoire, Novotel, Hilton Hotel, and Hotel du Golfe. The largest, oldest, and best known gallery in Côte d'Ivoire is the Rose d'Ivoire situated in the basement of the Hotel Ivoire in the Cocody quarter of Abidjan.[26] The Rose d'Ivoire was established in the 1960s and originally run by an East Indian family.[27] It is now owned and operated by an expatriate French dealer. The gallery contains most of the same items which are available in the market places. Unlike the market place, however, a price tag is affixed to each item. A staff of about four African salesmen, each robed in identical blue smocks, are always available to answer a buyer's questions. The salesmen never push a client toward making a purchase, they are simply there to respond to inquiries, remove objects that are exhibited in locked cases, and ring up an occasional sale at the register. I would argue that this unobtrusive, non-aggressive form of behavior is in fact a calculated sales tactic; the whole idea of the gallery is to provide the buyer with an alternative to the bustle and confusion of the outdoor market place.

Although it tries to differentiate itself from the market place, the gallery bears certain structural similarities to those observed in outdoor vending arenas. Like the Plateau market place, for example, the Rose d'Ivoire is

7 Hausa storehouse-owners with children. Treichville quarter, Abidjan, July
1988.

organized and structured around thresholds of secrecy that are meant to attest to different levels of authenticity, various ranges of price, and different claims about investment value. The main room of the gallery is stocked with replicas or copies which are intended largely for hotel guests, tourists, business travelers, and other casual buyers. An alcove at the back corner of the main gallery is filled with better quality, more expensive, and more carefully crafted replicas. It also contains a small selection of older, used objects (mainly furniture, musical instruments, and household items). Across from this recessed area in the main basement gallery is a locked room containing what are presented to the buyer as fine, rare, and "authentic" objects. Two tiny, plexi-covered windows cut into walls at opposite ends of the room allow prospective buyers to peer rather uncomfortably into the locked chamber. Those wishing to enter the room, however, need to get a salesman to unlock the door; the salesman is required to wait inside while the customer looks around. Masks, statues, decorated heddle pulleys, staffs, and some traditional weapons set out on the surface of a huge wooden Senufo funerary bed are displayed in this room. These are the three areas which are designed for public consumption. Access to each level requires an ever greater degree of inquisitiveness on the part of the consumer. Finally, a fourth level of secrecy with cautiously restricted access is located in a room adjacent to the owner's private office which is one floor above the basement store.[28] One evening, two French collectors and I were ushered into the inner sanctum. In a cramped room, where a tiny air conditioning duct battled the intense heat of track lighting, the owner and his prospective clients sat in leather armchairs analyzing the aesthetic merit of various *objets d'art* which lined the four walls of the room. In a secret compartment hidden behind a panel in one of the walls is a locked combination safe. Within the safe, the owner told his guests, are the real "treasures" of the Rose d'Ivoire, some of which are protected in their own felt bag. Many of these objects are from the owner's private collection. However, he was quick to inform the prospective buyers, they are all available for sale – if the price is right.

A second private gallery in Abidjan is the Galerie Pokou which is owned and operated by a Lebanese dealer who has spent a lifetime in Côte d'Ivoire. The gallery requires a brief mention here simply because of its unique approach to the presentation of its objects. Unlike the Rose d'Ivoire, the Galerie Pokou does not generally cater to tourists or casual buyers. It is located in Marcory, a remote part of suburban Abidjan, on a side street which is difficult to find. The gallery is housed in a room of the owner's estate. About twenty objects are displayed on glass bookshelves and in small niches recessed into a stucco wall. This "semi-public" room of the gallery was only opened in 1987.[29] This part of the gallery is intended, according to the owner, to attract some mid-level collectors to his store. The main focus of the business, however, are the

8 "Marchand d'Objets d'Arts Africains" art gallery and souvenir shop outside Hotel Les Cascades. Man, June 1988.

up-scale objects which are sold from the owner's sitting room. Like the levels
of secrecy built into the Rose d'Ivoire, the Galerie Pokou constructs a level of
secrecy by allowing the buyer to gain access to the owner's "private" quarters.
Six pedestals (each with its own spot light and rotating platform) are arranged
in different corners of the living room. Sipping an aromatic blend of Lebanese
coffee, the owner tries to ascertain the buyer's preferences with regard to style,
genre, object type, price range, etc. He then goes to a backroom – which is
strictly off limits to outsiders *and* anthropologists – and emerges with several
samples of the type of art in which the client has expressed interest, displaying
each object on its own stand. Unlike the Rose d'Ivoire, there are no prices
posted on these objects. Prices are stated verbally. Some bargaining or price
negotiation occurs, however, it does not follow the same pattern as bargaining
in the market places (see Chapter 3).[30]

Roadside stalls

Along the side of the road leading beyond the Abidjan airport at Port Bouët and
toward the ex-colonial capital of Grand Bassam is about a half-mile stretch of
covered roadside stalls (Plate 9). The stalls cater primarily to expatriates and
tourists driving east from Abidjan toward the resort beaches and hotels located

along the Atlantic coast. Most of the stalls are owned by Senegalese merchants; some, however, are run by Ivoirians. Many of the same contemporary objects which are available in the Abidjan market places are sold from the roadside stalls. In addition, however, the stalls sell a few items which are manufactured on site and, for the most part, are not available anywhere else. Among these items are the works of Anoh Acou, a Baule artist who creates wooden carvings of Western household items (shoes, suits, radios, telephones, etc.).[31] Because he sells his carvings directly from one of the roadside stalls, Anoh Acou is able to avoid the middlemen in the urban market places. Another art form, which is manufactured and sold at the roadside stalls outside Grand Bassam, are cotton textile belts and sashes. These items are created by a group of weavers who work on narrow-band horizontal looms in the back area of the stalls. They are woven in brightly colored threads and displayed on large wooden racks along the side of the road. A small group of artists from Ghana, headed by a man named Ringo, sell wooden airplanes, helicopters, buses, cars, and boats fabricated from scrap lumber and colored with brilliant enamel paints. Most of these artists are highly independent entrepreneurs who have no interest in dealing with the market-place middlemen. They have been very successful in selling their work from their roadside stalls, and, on their own, have been able to market their goods to a number of art and craft galleries in New York City. Finally, a number of the roadside stalls sell bamboo and rattan furniture (chairs, couches, tables, lamps, etc.) which are made on site by local craftsmen. Most of these items are purchased by expatriates for furnishing their Abidjan homes.

Beach vendors

Although it makes up a relatively small portion of the overall art market in Côte d'Ivoire, some art is sold by ambulant vendors who walk up and down the beach hawking their wares to sunbathing expatriates and tourists. Some of these vendors are small-scale Wolof traders, many of whom are young boys who are not able to sell on their own in Abidjan. They deal largely in small wooden drums (*tam tam*), roughly hewn Akan fertility dolls (*akuaba*), various styles of bracelets and necklaces, and carved wooden penises. Curiously, the beach is one of the few places where this last item is sold. They are usually kept hidden inside the vendor's robe pocket or in a plastic bag; when they are proffered to the Western buyer, they are revealed with a great show of mock secrecy.

The largest group of itinerant beach vendors are migrant Tuaregs from Mali and Niger. Dressed in their customary blue robes and headwraps, they walk up and down the beaches selling leather-covered boxes or trunks and leather sheathed swords and knives. Most of the boxes are made by the vendors themselves in Abidjan. A recent innovation is the manufacturing of boxes which

9 "Galerie Bassamoise" roadside stall. Near Grand Bassam, October 1987.

have been designed with individual partitions to accommodate either audio or video cassettes. Because of the strict regulation of trade in the urban market places, the beach is one of the few areas where the Tuareg craftsmen are allowed to sell directly to Western buyers.

Classification of goods

At this point, it may be helpful to classify the range of goods which traders sell in the market places. The typology which I propose combines the trader's own classification of object types with the prevalent social scientific typology of commoditized forms of art (Graburn 1976, 1984; Richter 1980).[32]

Antiquités

Objects which the traders classify as *antiquités* include items which were made for indigenous use but have become commodities and found their way into the art market. This is the category of goods which interests serious (i.e., investment-oriented) African art collectors and dealers. When sold in Abidjan, these type of items are generally found in the wooden trunks at the back of the market place, in the storehouses and homes in Treichville quarter, as well as in permanent galleries.

Antiquités enter the market at a slow place and on a piecemeal basis. First, an *antiquité* can be brought directly to the market place by the owner or another villager.[33] Objects (that are either stolen or bought in a community) sometimes arrive in the hands of high school or university students returning to Abidjan from school vacations spent in their village. Sellers such as these have very little idea what an object is actually worth, and when the piece is brought into the market place traders will usually criticize it saying that it is neither good nor really old. After extended haggling and verbal humiliation the object is usually purchased by a trader for the lowest possible price.[34] Second, an object can be obtained in a village by a local carver. Aware of the economic value of an old mask or statue, artists sometimes offer to substitute a replica in exchange for the original. These pieces are sold to traders in the larger towns who then transport them to Abidjan. Finally, the bulk of the *antiquités* that enter the market are collected by professional traders who wander on foot or bicycle from village to village searching for art. Objects collected in this manner are obtained largely through barter – exchanged for imported enamelware basins, machetes, pressure lamps, sugar, and cloth.

Although it would be difficult to inventory a complete stock of such items, it is nonetheless possible to identify a certain range of object types. Items in this category include: wooden face masks (a majority of which are from Côte d'Ivoire, Burkina Faso, Mali, Liberia, Guinea, and a smaller number from Sierra Leone, Nigeria, Cameroon, Zaire); metal masks (Senufo brass and aluminum *kpélié*); fiber masks (Senufo and Dogon); miniature masks (Dan and Mano); wooden statues and statuettes (a very large portion of which are Lobi, Baule, Senufo, but also Agni, Attié, Koulango, Bété, Dan from Côte d'Ivoire and others from Burkina Faso, Mali, Liberia, Ghana, Togo, Nigeria, Cameroon, Zaire); musical instruments (flutes, whistles, rattles, iron gongs with wooden clappers, anklets and bracelets with bells, drums, xylophones, blowing horns, string kora); weaving implements (beater bars, shuttles, pulleys, heddles, weaving swords, spindle whorls); household items (spoons, ladles, pestles, clay and wooden pipes, medical equipment, canes and walking sticks, flywhisks, slingshots, whips, gameboards, iron currencies, iron lamps, ladders, fishing gaffs, animal traps and nets, granary doorlocks, storage baskets, bowls, containers, bags); furniture (chairs, stools, beds); personal adornment (combs, hairpins, bracelets, necklaces, rings, earrings, hats, head-dresses, shoes and sandals, pubic aprons); goldweighing equipment (brass weights, scales, measuring spoons, sieves, storage boxes); ironsmithing instruments (pliers, bellows, anvils); weapons (bows and arrows, quivers, knives, swords, axes, spears, clubs, antique European and Arab-made rifles and hand guns); ritual objects (divination boards, oracle boxes, funerary vessels, pendants, amulets, circumcision knives); regalia items (staffs, finials, ceremonial flywhisks, crowns); textiles (tie-and-dye fabrics, narrow-band cloths, hunter's tunics).

Copies

Copies, sometimes known in the literature as "commercial fine arts," "replicas" or "pseudo-traditional" arts, are defined here as art-forms which imitate traditional forms of art but are produced expressly for sale to outsiders. These types of objects are made for eventual sale although they adhere to culturally embedded aesthetic and formal standards. *Copies* are sold both in the front and in the back of urban market places, from storehouses, galleries, roadside stalls, and beaches. They are sometimes marketed as replicas, but also have the potential of being sold as *antiquités* – depending on the seller's assessment of the buyer's knowledge of African art. Included in this category are: wooden face masks (primarily carved in the style of the four major art producing ethnic groups in Côte d'Ivoire – Baule, Guro, Senufo, Dan – as well as in the styles of some other groups within Côte d'Ivoire and from other West and Central African nations); miniature masks (Dan, but also Guéré, Senufo, Baule); statues and statuettes (Baule, Senufo, Asante, Fante, and Lobi among others); goldweights (geometric and figurative) and measuring spoons; gameboards; musical instruments (drums, xylophones, string kora with brass or cowrie decorations); bronze casts of royal portrait heads from Benin and Ife; wooden display combs (Asante); Tuareg leather boxes and embroidered saddle bags, as well as leather handled and sheathed swords and daggers; Tuareg silver and silver-alloy jewelry (bracelets, *croix d'Agadez* pendants, earrings); leather-covered Fulani herding hats.

Nyama-nyama

"When the profit motive or the economic competition of poverty override aesthetic standards," writes Nelson Graburn, "satisfying the consumer becomes more important than pleasing the artist. These are often called 'tourist' arts or 'airport' arts and may bear little relation to traditional arts of the creator culture or to those of any other groups" (1976: 6). Many of these items are visual fictions bearing only minor resemblance to anything known in either the culture of production or consumption. This category of art sometimes glossed by traders as "*nyama-nyama*"[35] is marketed almost exclusively to foreign tourists, business travelers, and expatriates. Serious collectors of African art hold these objects in disdain, viewing them, as Price puts it "as a ruse perpetrated by wily natives" (1989: 79). Included in this category are: a number of "invented" sculptural genres (among the most popular are the so-called "skeleton" figures carved in Senufo style); masks (the most noteworthy are the circular Luba/Songye-inspired masks which are inlaid with brass, beads, and shells);[36] small brass figurative statues (lost-wax casts in the form of musicians, women carrying head loads, farmers with hoes, etc., as well as figures representing enlarged goldweight motifs and so-called "pornographic" weights, known in the local trade as *bétisses*); ivory bracelets and necklaces (both pure white ones which are marketed as new, and those which are stained dark with tea or henna and marketed as "antiques"); ivory figures (animals, female busts, carved horns); malachite jewelry (necklaces, bracelets, earrings); malachite carvings (mainly animals, small lidded boxes, and carved chess pieces and boards); both ebony and "fake" ebony (i.e., a light wood stained with dark dyes) figures carved in the form of wild animals (elephant, antelope, giraffe, bird) or humans (generally a profile bust of a female with elaborate coiffure); cowrie-covered belts and bracelets; beaded bracelets from Mali; painted mud cloths from Korhogo; ice buckets and small "cocktail" dishes made from carved coconut shells; cups with painted floral designs made from shafts of bamboo; throw pillow covers embroidered with designs of animals and masks; shoes, handbags, wallets, and belts made from alligator, snake, and other reptilian skins; dyed leather sandals from Mali and Niger; woven straw hats.

Western-derived art forms

Western-derived art forms are defined here as items which are conceived within "European traditions, but in content express feelings totally different [and] appropriate to the new cultures" (Graburn 1976: 7). This is the smallest category of objects sold in the market. In the Plateau market place, there were a handful of oil paintings on canvas representing village and pastoral scenes; some "sand paintings" made by pouring different colors of sand over patches of white glue; and some repoussé copper plaque designs. In all my time in the market place, I never saw a single one of these objects sold (for a sensitive discussion of the difficulties of marketing this category of art, see Jules-Rosette 1990).

Supply and distribution

Objects sold in the various Côte d'Ivoire art markets are obtained from a number of different sources. Some items are acquired from itinerant traders or carriers who hunt through rural villages for anything that can be resold into the art market. A small percentage of objects are acquired directly from villagers who bring art objects to market vendors. Some items are purchased from agents who, acting as representatives of artists (or groups of artists), transport recently manufactured objects from rural or suburban artisanal workshops to urban

10 Artisanal workshop. Port de Carena, Abidjan, June 1988.

market places (Plate 10). Finally, some objects are purchased directly by market vendors who themselves travel to rural towns and villages purchasing from local traders and local artists.

Although they often claim to buyers (especially tourists) that they themselves purchased an object from a village owner, in no case was I able to find an urban market trader who himself travels through rural areas buying artifacts from village sources. The persistence and energy necessary to establish village-level contacts and supply networks is incompatible with the time which is required for selling merchandise in the market places. Since they cannot afford to wait for the highest price, those who supply art from village sources must sell their merchandise with only a small margin of profit. And since they cannot afford the time to search through villages for art, those who sell art in the market places must rely on professional intermediaries for their supply of goods.

Intermediate mobile traders (many of whom are of Hausa, Djerma, or Dioula ethnicity) travel from village to village in search of whatever they think they can sell to merchants of art in any of the larger towns of Côte d'Ivoire, as well as in Abidjan itself. Itinerant traders are organized in informal groups that specialize in particular geographic regions. Among the Baule, for example, Hausa traders are centered around the towns of Bouaké and Dimbokro; among the Senufo, traders congregate in and around the town of

Korhogo; among the Dan, traders work both out of the towns of Man and Danané.

When they are ready to go out on their searches for art, the traders radiate from a central town to the surrounding villages. Most of the traders return again and again to the same villages, and to many of the same individuals within these villages, in order to inquire about the status of particular objects which they may be in the process of negotiating.[37] Some itinerant merchants communicate in the local language. Many of those who work in central-west Ghana, for instance, speak Asante. Traders who do not speak a local language must communicate in a lingua franca, which in most regions of Côte d'Ivoire is Dioula. Many of the traders, however, who are not competent in a local language, or those who are unfamiliar with a certain village, will use villagers as "guides" to local sources of art. In some cases these guides are village youths who have secret knowledge of where objects are stored in the village community.[38] In other cases, these local-level guides are village carvers who know the location of older objects – e.g., those which either they or another artist they know carved in the past. By negotiating through a local artist, traders are sometimes able to acquire an old figure or mask with the understanding that the carver will provide a replica for local use.[39]

Itinerant suppliers arrive in Abidjan alone or in small groups of two or three. Many of the Hausa/Djerma traders stay in Abobo quarter, a residential neighborhood to the north of Abidjan proper. Once they have arrived with their goods, informal networks of communication inform some of the merchants at the Plateau market place that the itinerant suppliers are in town. Being informed of this arrival is extremely important for the trader since supplies are limited and they must be quick in seeking out the objects. As one trader told me, after having an argument with a customer, "I would much rather lose a customer than a supplier. New customers can always be found, but regular suppliers are very hard to find" (1/29/88). Even though most suppliers, in the particular network which I studied, were Hausa, they showed very little preference in their trading practices to other Hausa merchants. Money, in this case, speaks louder than ethnicity. When they would arrive in Abidjan, for example, the Hausa suppliers would not inform the Hausa traders in preference to the non-Hausa. In fact, one of the most successful buyers from the Hausa suppliers was Asan Diop, a Wolof trader from Senegal. Because he was a good client who "paid well," he was among the first that the Hausa suppliers would notify when they arrived in town. And, furthermore, since he was one of the few market-place traders who drove a motorcycle, one of the fastest means of transportation through the crowded streets of Abidjan, he was usually able to arrive in Abobo quarter before anyone else.

In some rural-urban West African market systems, such as the cattle market in Nigeria which was studied in the 1960s by Abner Cohen, itinerant suppliers have a personal relationship with an urban "landlord"[40] who lodges, feeds, and entertains the suppliers when they arrive in the city. The landlord uses his own distribution networks to sell the cattle which the suppliers have brought, and after a few weeks, the landlord pays the suppliers the price which had been negotiated for the cattle (Cohen 1965; Hill 1966).

No such arrangement exists between the art traders and art suppliers. The suppliers reside with kin involved in other commercial pursuits, or if they have no such contacts they simply stay at inexpensive hotels. When Abdurrahman Madu, for example, a stallholder in the Plateau market place in Abidjan, travels to other urban centers in Côte d'Ivoire, he does not stay in the homes of the local traders from whom he buys. He prefers to stay in hotels. "They invite me to stay with them, but if you accept then it becomes too complicated. What if you can't agree on a price. If he has put you up in his home, it is much more difficult to bargain. Maybe he has nothing I even want to buy. I don't want to feel obliged to buy something" (12/1/87).

The difference between the arrangements which exist for the cattle market versus those for the art market can be explained largely by the difference in the nature of the merchandise which is being exchanged. Although there may be some variability in the quality of cattle within a single herd, the difference in quality is rather negligible.[41] In the art market, however, especially where *antiquités* are concerned, there is a huge difference in quality and value among the various items which are bought and sold. Since the quality of goods is so unpredictable, contractual agreements and trading partnerships are more risky and therefore less profitable.

2   The division of labor and the management of capital

> If the division of labor produces solidarity, it is not only because it makes each individual an *exchangist*, as the economists say; it is because it creates among men an entire system of rights and duties which link them together in a durable way.
>
> Emile Durkheim, *The Division of Labor in Society* (1933) [1893]

The type of traders who sell art in the Côte d'Ivoire art market range from large-scale owners of supply storehouses with a high-investment inventory of several thousand objects, to the petty street vendors who own virtually no stock at all.[1] The different types of traders cater to a whole range of foreign consumers, ranging from wholesale purchasers who ship entire sea freight containers of African art from Côte d'Ivoire to European or American ports of trade, to the vacationing tourists or business travelers interested in acquiring only one or two souvenirs.

Unlike other sectors of the West African market economy which are largely dominated by women traders (e.g., the cloth, vegetable, and prepared food trades), the art market is almost exclusively a male domain (cf. Mintz 1971: 257). The predominance of men can be attributed to several different factors. First, many of the supply networks for the art trade have grown out of traditional commercial routes, especially those controlled by Hausa merchants (see Amselle 1977; Lovejoy 1980; Grégoire 1992). Since these older trades (e.g., the kola nut trade) were largely male-oriented forms of commerce (except see Gnobo 1976), the art trade has remained in the hands of male traders. Second, and perhaps of greater significance, is the fact that many of the arts which the traders handle are considered to be the property of men. In the village context, for instance, most masks and figural statues are carved by men, owned by men, and in some cases are even forbidden to be seen by women and children. Although many of the arts which traders sell are not considered sacred (but rather contemporary copies made exclusively for the trade) the male-centered perspective which characterizes the "traditional" arts still predominates. Finally, the Syndicat des Antiquaires, which licenses all legitimate art trade in Côte d'Ivoire, does not permit women to join in their membership. This, however, is more the result of this gendered division of labor than its cause.

The role of women

The only cases of female participation in the art trade with which I am familiar, involve long-distance suppliers of art from parts of Côte d'Ivoire and other West African nations. Like most exceptions, these few cases involving women's participation in the commerce of art are particularly illuminating, and throw light on some profound assumptions about the division of labor by gender in the African art market.

Bembe Aminata is a supplier of Dan dolls (*poupées Dan*) from the region of Man in western Côte d'Ivoire (Plate 11).[2] About once a month, she travels by public transportation with a supply of Dan dolls (approximately 200 stuffed into burlap sacs) from Man to Abidjan. She obtains the dolls on credit from the craftsmen who make them at various workshops in and around the towns of Man and Danané (see Bouabré 1987a: 11). In Abidjan, she sells the dolls on short-term credit to the market-place traders. After distributing the dolls to traders at both the Plateau and Cocody market places,[3] Aminata waits for up to thirty days to collect her money. Although no trader could sell all the dolls he had obtained within the thirty-day period of credit, he is usually able to raise the necessary cash from the sale of other objects in his stock.

While in Abidjan, Aminata visits the market places almost every day – socializing with the traders and subtly reminding them, through her presence, that she is still waiting to be paid. She is housed on the outskirts of Abidjan with her husband's family. I never witnessed a case where Aminata took back the dolls from a trader who had defaulted on his credit by not paying for the goods within the thirty-day period. Often, I saw her stay longer than thirty days in order to collect. In one instance, I noted that she left Abidjan without having collected from a particular trader (who was unable to raise enough money, but promised to pay her the moment she got back).

Another woman who was involved at the supply end of the market was Kwasi Adja, an English-speaking Asante woman from Ghana who transported carvings from a craft workshop in the Asante capital of Kumase in west-central Ghana. Her brother is one of the carvers from the Kumase workshop.[4] Unlike Aminata, Adja did not stay in Abidjan for a month at a time. She required payment from her buyers within three or four days. She took back objects from those who did not pay.

Women who have no formal ties to the art trade are sometimes used as couriers on an informal basis by traders from other parts of West Africa. A trader from Bamako, for example, sent two women – who were on their way to Abidjan to visit relatives – with a shipment of Bamana antelope figures (*chi wara*). The women traveled by public bus with the objects packed in sacs. The figures were delivered to a Plateau market-place trader who had ordered the pieces from his "brother" in Mali. When asked why women were involved in the supply of workshop artifacts to Abidjan markets, all the traders (including the women suppliers themselves) responded that women could cross border patrols with greater ease than men and, therefore, were less likely to get "taxed," harassed, or have their goods confiscated.[5]

Recently, a number of Guinean women have been arriving in New York City with cargo loads of African art. They come to the United States to buy video recorders, televisions, and radios for resale in Africa. Their goal in selling the art is not to turn a direct profit, but rather to finance the purchase of electronic equipment through a short-term credit arrangement. That is to say, they take the art in Guinea on credit from workshop artists, they sell the art at (or near) cost, and then use the cash to buy electronics in New York. Their profit, therefore, is turned in Africa on the sale of Western goods rather than in the West on the sale of African goods.

Some of the New York based male art traders blame these women for the sluggish African art market which currently exists in the United States.[6] "Women, unlike men, will sell their merchandise at any price," said Malam Yaaro. "They don't have what it takes to wait for a reasonable amount of money. It's because of them that things are not working anymore in New York" (3/14/92). Since the veteran New York traders know that the women have to return to Africa as quickly as possible (to turn their profit on the electronics and to pay their debt to the art producers), they will negotiate to buy a woman's entire shipment of art for substantially below market value.[7] The traders who buy from the women can then pass on the savings to their American clients, thereby squeezing out their competition who cannot afford to sell at such low prices, and ultimately driving down the market value of certain object types. This process, according to some of the New York based traders, has resulted in a deflationary trend in the American market for African art, so that objects which once sold easily for $80 or $100, now sell for as little as $30 or $40.

Hierarchy of traders

The men who sell art in the African market system can be classified according to criteria of wealth, power, and reputation. Far from being a homogenous group of entrepreneurs, art traders draw either obvious or subtle distinctions of class and status among themselves. Although it may not always be clear to the outside observer where a particular person fits into the hierarchy of African art traders, the men themselves are acutely aware of their social position – each aspiring through prayer and action for upward mobility and greater respect.

11 Dan doll with painted wooden face and costume made of cotton cloth, raphia fibers, feathers, wool yarn, and fur. Height 29 cm. Private collection. Photograph by Richard Meier.

Storehouse owners

The main storehouses in Abidjan are located in the African residential neighborhood of Treichville quarter. Two avenue blocks of Treichville (roughly at the intersection of Avenues 11 and 12) are lined with warehouse-style storefronts whose interiors are often overflowing with a huge variety of heaped or stacked objects of art. Sitting outdoors on wooden chairs or squatting on goat-skin mats, drinking tonic water or heavily sweetened tea, storehouse owners and their assistants spend the day waiting for either buyers or suppliers to arrive at their stores.

The inside of a storehouse usually consists of a jumbled array of objects which have been accumulated over a period of many years (Plate 12). The scene is not unlike one which Geertz described for the Moroccan bazaar: "an accumulation of material objects [which] God himself could not inventory, and some of which He could probably not even identify . . . sensory confusion brought to a majestic pitch" (1979: 197). The sense of disarray in the store-house is, at least in part, the result of abandon, but it is also a calculated way in which a trader creates the impression that buried inside his storehouse may be a real treasure. One Abidjan-based American collector told me that he liked spending hours in the storehouses, digging through piles of "neglected" art. "Most of these guys," he said, "don't even know what they have in there" (11/15/87). When I related this idea to the traders, they were delighted. "Do you really think we would leave a good piece buried at the bottom of a pile? We know that what is there is no good, but if someone thinks there are treasures in there, that is good for our business" (12/2/87).[8]

Although the storehouses contain largely objects which the traders consider to be of inferior quality,[9] they provide one of the few instances in the art market where storage and accumulation are possible. Many African traders – whether in art or in other commodities – lack the necessary capital to store their goods in order to wait for seasonal or unanticipated price increases.[10] Noticing the rapid increase in prices for so-called "colonial" carvings (see Chapter 6), one trader told me that he knew if he held on to some of these statues for a few years he could probably make a much higher profit. However, he said that he could not afford the luxury of not selling. He needed a quick turnover to recuperate his invested capital with only a modest margin of profit.[11]

Market-place stallholders

In all three market places in Abidjan, the rights to stalls are strictly controlled by the municipal government. Stalls (or smaller spaces within a stall) must be rented from the Abidjan City Hall. The fee, which is collected on a weekly basis, ranges from 200 CFA (50 cents) to 1,500 CFA ($5). In exchange for this

12 Interior view of an art storehouse. Treichville quarter, Abidjan, November 1987.

fee, the City Hall provides a small amount of security (occasional guard patrols at night) and cleans the market space on a more-or-less regular basis.[12]

Most stallholders begin their careers as assistants or apprentices. Some are sent as young boys from their natal village or home country to work for a relative in Abidjan. By selling to tourists and foreign buyers, the young men begin to learn the routines of the market place – the networks of supply, the range and quality of art forms, the tactics of successful bargaining, and the tastes and preferences of the consumers. Eventually they may be left in charge of the stall, while the owner conducts business out of his home or storehouse. And, later they may be given complete responsibility for the stall – buying stock-in-trade, paying stall fees, etc. (Plate 13).

Within the market place there is a constant tension between competition and cooperation. Because of the way the market place is laid out (with stalls grouped closely together along adjoining paths), and because of the high degree of similarity among the merchandise which is being bought and sold, traders are always in economic rivalry with one another.[13] In the tourist trade – where there is a limited range of variability in product type and quality – most merchants are selling roughly the same sort of goods which they have purchased at about the same price. In other sectors of the African market economy (e.g., fruits and vegetables), traders handle daily competition by relying on the business of regular customers. Traders create their own body of repeat-customers by extending credit (Mintz 1961, 1964a; Lewis 1976). Because traders in the art market cater largely to tourists and other transients, the art traders (at the level of the tourist trade at least) can neither rely on the business of a return clientele nor on the patronage of indebted buyers.

Competition in the art market comes not only from external rivals but also from within a business enterprise itself. Most multi-trader stalls (where a stall-holder hires one or more assistants or apprentices) tend toward fragmentation as employees turn into entrepreneurs who run their own affairs within the framework of their employer's business (cf. Fanselow 1990: 258). In the Plateau market place, for example, Barane M'Bol was employed by his uncle to sell at one of the market-place stalls. M'Bol, however, was also active surreptitiously in seeking out his own clients in the street, he was engaged in credit and commission sales with other traders, and he bought objects on his own from itinerant suppliers. Although he did not pay for the stall right and was not responsible for the management of a large stock-in-trade, he used his position to his own advantage, in such a way that he was inevitably under-cutting his employer's earnings.

Door-to-door vendors

Many of the storehouse owners have what one trader called, "a small army of young men," who sell art door-to-door to a large Abidjan expatriate clientele. These ambulant traders or, what are sometimes called in the literature, circuit-traders, take goods on credit (see below) from the storehouse owners and ply their wares both at the homes of expatriate clients and, less frequently, to some of the stallholders in the market places.[14] Depending on a customer's generosity and tendency to buy, foreigners who have become integrated into the urban network are visited by at least three or four salesmen a month.[15] Working alone or in groups of two to three, traders generally arrive at a customer's home with several bags of art. Some of the traders have their own cars, most of them, however, travel by taxi, while some of the less prosperous must carry their heavy loads on foot or by public transportation. Occasionally, traders phone their clients ahead to set up appointments, often, however, they simply show up at the client's doorstep – and must sometimes wait up to half a day before they are even received in the person's home.[16] Some clients invite the traders into their homes, others receive traders on the veranda, driveway, or lawn. At an orientation meeting organized by the American Embassy in Abidjan, a speaker told the new arrivals that for security reasons art traders should not be invited inside their homes. Some non-diplomatic collectors, who do not consider the traders to be a security risk, do not allow merchants to enter their homes for different reasons. First, collectors often do not want the

13 Market-place stallholder with his stock of merchandise. Man, June 1988.

vendors to see their collections, for they might have objects in their possession which were bought from rival traders.[17] Second, a collector might not let a door-to-door vendor into his home for fear that the trader might spread the word that the collector has a certain object in his possession. If a collector sells to other collectors (via the intermediary of an African trader) he would not want the people to whom he sells to know that he owns certain objects which he may eventually want to put on the market.

One example of this tactic is illustrated by François Dupont, an account executive for a French-owned bank in Abidjan. Several years after having been assigned to the Abidjan branch of the bank for which he worked in Paris, Dupont began collecting Akan goldweights. At first, when traders brought him newly arrived lots of weights, he would carefully choose what he felt were the best pieces. He would negotiate a price for the objects he had selected, and the trader would then sell the rest of the lot to other collectors or African traders. Eventually, Dupont says, he realized that because he was picking out what (both he and the trader felt) were the best pieces in the lot, he was essentially paying for the entire lot. Whatever the trader sold after he left Dupont's house was above and beyond what he thought he could get for the whole lot. Therefore, rather than select choice objects, Dupont began purchasing entire lots of goldweights. He would retain the pieces he wanted and would place the rest of the weights on the market. Since he was European, however, it would have been awkward (or, in his words, "demeaning") to go door-to-door to his collector friends and sell the weights. Therefore, he entered into an agreement with a single African trader who acted as his agent in the resale of goldweights which he did not want for his collection. The trader was given a price, and he made his profit from whatever he could get above that price. Dupont sold a number of his weights to a well-established Lebanese dealer in Abidjan. According to Dupont, if the Lebanese dealer knew that the weights were coming from his collection he would probably never buy them.[18] To prevent him, and any other collectors or dealers, from gaining access to knowledge regarding his stock, Dupont only allowed a select group of traders into his home, and, furthermore, he never displayed his entire collection.

Street hawkers and stall assistants

At least half the people who are involved in the exchange of art in the Plateau market place are neither stallholders nor even the actual owners of the objects they try to sell. Many of the wealthier stallholders hire assistants to carry out the daily business of selling art to tourists and other foreign buyers. Some of the more prosperous stallholders who carry both souvenir and up-scale art often do not get involved directly selling to tourists. Although they are present nearly every day at their stall in the market place, they usually do not deal with customers unless someone is looking for *antiquités* or serious collectible art. They are also present in the event that a supplier should happen to bring a shipment of goods into the market place.

In order to avoid bargaining with tourists, large-scale stallholders hire one or more apprentices who are paid a modest weekly salary, an occasional commission on a sale, and sometimes given a lunchtime meal. Many of these apprentices are members of the stallholder's extended family – relatives who have been sent to the city by family members, or relatives who have lost their jobs in the city (construction, transportation, etc.) and are looking for temporary employment until they can find another position in the urban labor force. If a stallholder's assistant happens not to be a direct relative, in every instance that I know he is at least a member of the same ethnic group. Wolofs will always hire other Wolofs, Hausas will hire other Hausas, Dioulas will hire other Dioulas, etc. Stall assistants do not always become professional traders. If they have the opportunity, many of them would favor moving on to other sectors of urban employment.

Although they do not purchase objects themselves, stall assistants are familiar with the appropriate retail price for the type of objects stocked in the stalls where they work. Their knowledge, however, of the symbolism, meaning, and history of African art is generally minimal. Successful assistants increase their number of sales by picking up from other traders the stories which are told about different types of objects (cf. Chapter 6). The measure of an assistant's accomplishment depends on his aggressiveness in the market place and in his ability to "catch" tourists. When buyers visit the market place there is an unwritten rule which prevents other vendors from intruding and starting competitive bargaining or trying to distract the buyer (cf. Malinowski and de la Fuente 1985: 63). In F. G. Bailey's language (1969), however, one might say that like players engaged in a game with agreed upon rules, traders modify and contest the boundaries of cooperative behavior.

During the rainy season the Plateau market place floods quickly after a storm. Pathé Diop's stall, which is on the outer perimeter of the market place, has a tendency to get completely surrounded by a huge puddle of rainwater. Diop decided to place a wooden plank across the flooded area so that his customers could walk up to his stall. Because the plank was very narrow, however, customers could not turn around and leave if Diop was standing behind them. "This is good for my business," said Diop, "because the tourists can't walk away from my stall" (7/14/88). Some of the traders complained that the plank was an unfair means by which to monopolize a group of buyers. "When they come in [to the market place] they get stuck in that one area, and then we don't get a chance to show them our things" (7/14/88). Eventually, Diop agreed to lay down more planks so that others could simultaneously gain access to the area – without the tourists or the traders getting their feet wet.

Another means of pushing the rules of market-place competition, is to go outside the market with a handful of goods and approach tourists directly on the street before they enter the market arena. Wolof traders refer to this practice as *poroh-poroh*.[19] Using this technique, traders either sell directly on the street, or lure tourists back to their stalls in the market place.

Internal market peddlers

In the Plateau market place, a small number of marginal actors in the art market economy earn a meager livelihood as internal market peddlers. Their role consists of selling objects from the stock of one stallholder to another stallholder in the market place. If a stallholder needs to raise a small amount of cash in a hurry – e.g., to pay the rental fee on his stall to the stall-right collector from the *mairie*, to buy a desirable object from an itinerant supplier, to repay an overdue loan which may have come to term through sudden social pressure, or simply to buy himself a midday meal – he may choose to liquidate one or more objects from his stock. Usually he selects an object which has been in his inventory for some time. Often, the seller may not even remember how much he originally paid for the item.

In order to liquidate an object or small portion of stock, the stallholder gives the item(s) to one of the internal market peddlers with whom he usually deals.[20] The trader sets a price (which is always low and often well below the normal price range for a particular type of object). The internal market peddler walks through the market place calling out the type of object he has to sell. He tries to get anything above the owner's asking price.[21] Because all the other stall-holders know that the object is being sold inexpensively and fast, the peddler's profit tends to be very low. Stallholders call peddlers from one end of the market to the next. "Hey, let's see what treasures you have for us today," one trader said as he motioned with his hand for the peddler to come nearer (12/2/87). The stallholders treat the internal market peddlers with calculated disrespect – reminding them that they are merely hawkers as opposed to real merchants of art.

The internal market peddlers allow stallholders to acquire quickly small amounts of cash without "lowering" their status to the level of a petty hawker.[22] Even after persistent questioning by rival stallholders, a peddler will not reveal the source of the objects he sells. A stallholder's temporary financial problems are thus kept secret from other traders. In every instance of intra-market peddling which I have witnessed, the object was eventually sold. The peddler's charge, that is to say, was never returned unsold to its owner. The system, therefore, provides a proven means of raising a small amount of cash in a hurry.

On becoming an art trader

Some of the traders have a childhood background in Qur'anic education (undertaken in their native country under the tutelage of a *marabout*) which enables them to read and write in Arabic script. Many can also read and write Roman numerals. Market-place traders who have frequent interaction with foreign buyers have a basic knowledge of spoken French. Some traders also speak a little English (which comes either from their interaction with tourists or from time spent in anglophone countries, such as Ghana or Nigeria). Unlike some other West African trade industries (e.g., the Hausa cattle market in Nigeria), none of the traders keep regular written accounts of their purchases, sales, or inventory (cf. Cohen 1965). Art merchants with a large stock-in-trade have an uncanny capacity to recall the price which they paid for nearly every object purchased within at least the last month, and often the past several years. They also have a keen memory for the objects which they themselves have handled – i.e., bought, sold, or simply seen. When a trader visits an expatriate collector's home, for instance, he can usually point out every object in the person's collection which has passed through his hands or which was offered to him for sale; he can recall from whom it was bought and for how much it was sold. When I showed some of the market-place traders a photographic book of carved West African slingshots, *Potomo Waka*, which had been published by a local Abidjan-based African art collector, many of them were able to recognize the slingshots which they (or one of their agents) had sold to the author of the book (see Chapter 5).

The success of an art trader depends on a combination of hard work, commercial acumen (which may include anything from knowing how to manage capital to developing a trained eye for quality art objects), prayer, and good fortune. This last variable, which accounts for the success of an art trader, is the one which is most talked about by the traders themselves. Good fortune is usually spoken of as a combination of luck and the will of God. If a trader makes a big sale, he will often kiss the money he receives (e.g., a 5,000 CFA note) and place the folded bill to his forehead. "Money brings money," they say. No matter how bad their business may be, traders find reassurance in the phrase *Dieu est grand* [God is great]. Lack of money, poor investments, and financial ruin are only considered temporary conditions in the life career of a trader. There is always the hope that the next day an itinerant supplier will bring a masterpiece (*une pièce "top"*)[23] to the market and sell it inexpensively. Or, there is the expectation that a foreign tourist or collector will buy something for far more money than it is usually worth. This is the faith which keeps a struggling trader in business – the glimmer of hope which enables him to open and close his market-place stall even if he has no more money in his pockets.

As Abdurrahman Madu put it, "It's like fishing . . . in the market you never know what you will catch" (1/29/88).

Many of the traders in the market place began as apprentices to their fathers, uncles, or some other male relative. Most of the stallholders seem to conceptualize art trading as a lifelong, full-time, permanent career. Many of the other merchants in the market place, however, simply consider trading as a temporary form of employment which provides a small amount of income until some more stable form of wage labor comes along.

A number of traders with whom I am acquainted entered the market through other forms of commerce. Bakayoko Ibrahim, for example, drives a truck with supplies of dried fish. He loads the dried fish from the ports in Abidjan and transports them to towns and villages in southern Burkina Faso and northern Ghana. Most of the regions where he sells fish are inhabited by members of the Lobi ethnic group. Because Lobi religion relies heavily on personal shrines made up of wooden sculptures and divination through carved figures, the Lobi people produce vast quantities of figural art (Meyer 1981). One of Ibrahim's cousins, who was himself an art trader in Ouagadougou, Burkina Faso, suggested that instead of returning from his fish-supplying trips with an empty truck, he should fill the truck with carvings which could then be sold in Abidjan. Ibrahim took his cousin's advice and began bringing back truck loads of Lobi sculpture. At first, he says, he bought anything he could find. Eventually, however, he developed an eye for quality in Lobi art and began buying pieces of greater value. He has been buying and selling Lobi art for the past ten years.[24]

When I met Ibrahim for the first time, he was sitting under the shade of a boabab tree in his family compound. Two of the six rooms in the compound are used for the storage of art. Ibrahim does not have a stall in any of the Abidjan market places. He sells to the stallholders, as well as to Western dealers who make their way to his compound (usually escorted by one of the market-place hawkers who is familiar with Ibrahim's "store"). It is unusual for traders to specialize – as Bakayoko Ibrahim has done – in the art of a single ethnic group, however, because of the circumstance under which Ibrahim collects the art, he is restricted to collecting in a single area among a single ethnic group. Thus, he is one of the few traders in the Côte d'Ivoire art market to have a genuine area specialty.[25]

Another trader who entered the market in a similar way as Bakayoko Ibrahim is Mulinde Robert. His transition to the art market, however, was sketched on a broader international scale. In 1976, Robert began coming to the United States from his native Nigeria to buy televisions, radios, and (eventually) video recorders. He shipped these objects to Nigeria where his brother sold them on the local market in Lagos. One of Robert's acquaintances in Nigeria, who was an art trader in one of the local tourist market places, suggested that since he already knew so much about international shipping, and already had so many useful contacts in the Nigerian customs service, that he begin shipping art from Nigeria to the United States. In the past several years, Robert has begun the importation of art. So far, his operation is of limited scale – i.e., transporting objects in his personal luggage on every trip he makes from Nigeria to the United States. Because he is not tied into the network of full-time African art traders in the United States, he does not have many clients and is, therefore, having trouble finding outlets for the objects which he transports.

After graduating from Qur'anic school, Malam Yaaro began his career as an Islamic religious specialist or *malam*. The *malamai* are a powerful group of mystical diviners and interpreters of Islam who draw upon Qur'anic scriptures and formulac with the goal of securing individual prosperity and good fortune for their clients (Cohen 1969: 165–70). A *malam* can help a person to get rich, to prosper in their trade, and to positively control their future. The *malamai*, however, do not get paid directly for their services, they must instead rely on the generosity of those they help. Not long after starting his career as a *malam*, Yaaro realized that those he helped were quickly getting rich while he remained poor. "Why should I keep praying for someone else to get rich?" Yaaro asked rhetorically, "It just didn't make any sense" (3/14/92). He chose, therefore, to leave the mystical world in order to reap directly the fruits of the material world. Through business connections he had made as a *malam*, he was able to enter the diamond industry in northern Côte d'Ivoire. Basing himself in the town of Korhogo, Yaaro would travel through remote villages buying mined diamonds from local diggers or organizing digs himself. His business expanded to the diamond mines of Ghana, where he would buy the precious minerals in order to export them to Liberia. In the late 1970s, however, Yaaro fell on hard times in the diamond market. Scrambling for a new profession, he was able to use his extant village connections in Côte d'Ivoire and Ghana to begin trading in art. The transition from diamonds to art was not an easy one for Malam Yaaro. Although the Hausa take pride in their business acumen and their monopoly over many different forms of commerce, the trade in African art objects represented a radical departure for Yaaro – an excursion into a world of "idols" and "fetishes" from which his intensive Qur'anic education had steered him away.[26] As he put it in one of our conversations:

I had left home to earn money, but I had no more job. I saw people making good money selling art. I knew God didn't approve of this kind of work, but in order to make money I got involved in the trade . . . When you have nothing and you need to eat you sometimes have to do things that God doesn't like. That's why I sell art even though I know God doesn't approve. (6/22/91)

Yaaro started to buy and sell in the regions of Korhogo and Accra. Within the last few years, he has expanded his business to the United States, where he now travels with a truck load of objects, selling art from New York to Los Angeles and most nearly everywhere in between. Before his first trip to America, Yaaro himself consulted a *malam* to insure a prosperous and successful journey. In discussing this consultation, Yaaro is quick to add, however, "I knew that when I would make money thanks to the blessings of the *malam*, I would repay him well for what he had done" (3/14/92).

There are a number of barriers that prevent people from becoming full-time traders (especially market-place traders). First, one must be admitted to the Syndicat des Antiquaires. Second, one must raise enough capital to purchase a market-place stall. Third, one must develop an eye for quality and a capacity for judging value and resale potential. One example of an unsuccessful bid to become a full-time trader in the market for *antiquités* is offered through the life history of Yusufu Tijjani, a thirty-two-year-old Hausa trader who now resides in the town of Korhogo. Tijjani has been selling African art since he was in his early twenties. He works for his father's brother, who is a well-established African art trader in northern Côte d'Ivoire. Tijjani recounted that when he first came to Korhogo, from his natal village in Niger, to work for his uncle, he tried to learn as much as he could about the trade and about the different types of artworks that his uncle bought and sold. When he himself had accumulated a little capital (from savings on commissions paid by his uncle) he began buying art directly from the itinerant suppliers. He displayed his goods alongside the objects he was selling for his uncle.

One day, he says, he purchased a Senufo rhythm pounder (*deble*) from one of the Dioula merchants who had just returned from the villages. "I really thought it was *top*," he said in an interview. He bargained for the piece, and agreed to pay the owner 40,000 CFA (about $130 in 1988). He left a deposit of 10,000 CFA and brought the piece to show his uncle. His uncle looked at the object and told him he had made a big error, that the piece was a recent copy, and that it was not worth anywhere near the price he had agreed to pay.[27] Tijjani tried to return the object to the supplier, but the merchant was not willing to give him back his deposit. So, Tijjani said, he returned the statue and forfeited the 10,000 CFA. "It was worth taking the loss in order to get rid of the thing," he said (6/6/88). Since this unfortunate incident, Tijjani has never bought anything on his own. He works strictly for his uncle, and sells mostly tourist pieces in front of the Mont Korhogo Hotel.

Credit, commissions, and capital

Unlike many other market systems in West Africa, the African art market is not structured around formal credit organizations or marketing cooperatives. One does not find, for instance, the rotating credit associations which are character- istic of many agricultural, produce, and textile markets. Nor does one find the large-scale money-lending institutions which, for instance, finance the cattle markets in various parts of West Africa. In the West African art market, credit is hard to come by, and capital is even harder to find. Most traders enter the African art business through kin relations – i.e., as helpers or assistants. From these relations, the traders gain the knowledge (e.g., the capacity to recognize quality objects and the ability to estimate appropriate object value) which is necessary to participate in the art trade. They also acquire enough stock-in-trade and capital to eventually branch off on their own.

One reason, I believe, that the art market does not follow a typical West African market strategy of money lending or credit relations (i.e., supplier-landlord-client associations) has to do with the nature of the commodities which the art traders buy and sell. In the *antiquités* trade, especially, the quality of objects varies so greatly, and the supply of first-rate items is so limited, that suppliers have no idea what they will find when they go into rural areas in search of resaleable goods. In the cattle markets, by contrast, the supply is known to both itinerant buyers and the landlords or intermediary brokers. If a supplier is given money on credit to bring cattle back to the city for a sponsoring landlord, both he and the landlord know pretty well what will be brought back. That is to say, from the broker's perspective, the investment is relatively secure. However, if a stallholder, gallery owner, or storehouse trader lent money to an itinerant supplier in the art market, he would have no way of knowing what the supplier will find – if anything at all. The cost of the trip, and the supply of manufactured goods with which to barter, would all be absorbed by the middleman who would have no guarantee on his investment.

The main problem, however, is also one of confidence. According to most of the traders whom I interviewed, the reluctance to finance suppliers or to form partnerships with specific suppliers is attributed to lack of trust.[28] Some traders say that the few times when they have given suppliers advances to purchase art, they discovered that the suppliers returned to Abidjan and sold *to other traders* whatever quality items they had found in the rural areas. After they had sold all they could, the suppliers would then go to their backers and report that they had not found very much. What accounts for this practice, according to the traders who have experimented with financing itinerant suppliers, is that the suppliers can make a larger profit by selling to traders with whom they have no financial or social debt. That is to say, if they brought all their goods to their backers, they would have to sell at a rate which took into account a monetary obligation. By selling to those who have not backed their trip, the suppliers can maximize their profit on the objects they have brought back, and at the same time capitalize on the defrayal of their purchase and travel costs.

Financial partnerships can be disadvantageous from both the backer's and the supplier's point of view. According to suppliers, they prefer to remain independent since there is always a chance that they will be able to buy a valuable item for very little money. If they were in a partnership, they would be obliged (at least in theory) to resell that item for less profit than they might otherwise be able to get. From the financier's perspective, fixed partnerships can also be detrimental. Again, because of the high degree of variability in the quality of items, traders prefer not to be obliged to buy from a set group of suppliers. They would rather have a wide field of suppliers with whom they do not have contractual obligations, and from whom they can purchase carefully selected items. Although credit is not common between suppliers and middle-men, credit relations do exist among traders within the resale market itself. At this level, the market system operates on several types of credit relations and systems of commission payment.

Market-place commissions

Traders who do not own either their own stall in the market place or their own stock of merchandise, can still participate in the trade as sellers or agents for other market-place traders. The profit they can derive from this type of participation is in the form of commissions or what traders refer to as *lèk*.[29] Market *lèk* is a kind of sales commission which allows traders who do not have enough capital with which to buy stock to still earn some money from the African art trade. As a tourist or group of tourists wanders through the market place, browsing at art objects in various stalls, there is usually at least one trader following the buyers from stall to stall, from one section of the market to another (Plate 14). Without knowing it, the tourists are crossing, at a brisk pace, scores of different lines of ownership. The trader accompanying the tourists through the market place becomes a sort of self-appointed "salesman," or as they are sometimes called in the literature "itinerant commission seller," who functions to bridge the different lines of ownership – creating an illusion that the market place is just like one big department store where you can pay for any item at any register. Rather than bargain with a number of different traders, the tourists deal only with "their" salesman. Traders say that this system is less confusing for the tourists, and, therefore, in the end, better for business.[30]

If a prospective buyer picks up an object which is the property of a given stall owner, the commission seller (rather than the owner of the stall) will conduct the bargaining. He usually knows the approximate value of an object, and so he will therefore conduct the bargaining without the help of the owner until the very last moment before the sale is finalized. If a successful sale appears to be imminent, then the commission seller will confirm the last price with the owner – speaking either in Dioula, Wolof, Hausa, or some other language which is presumably unintelligible to the tourist. After the customer is gone, the

14 European tourists negotiating a sale with Wolof traders at Plateau market place. Abidjan, December 1987.

commission seller must give to the owner the entire amount of cash earned from the sale. He will then demand his commission or *lèk*. The amount of the *lèk* which is paid is generally very small (100 to 1,000 CFA depending on the profit from the sale). The amount of the *lèk* is never fixed in relation to particular objects or to a particular sale price. For this reason, it is a value which is almost always vigorously contested.

Arguments erupt frequently in the market place about the payment of *lèk*. Stallholders may claim that their margin of profit was too small to give any significant amount of *lèk*. They may pay more or less *lèk* depending on their relationship to the commission seller (e.g., ethnic affiliation, friendship, etc.). I have witnessed several instances where a trader tried to hold back a seller's *lèk* altogether. These instances sometimes erupt into market-wide debates about stallholders and their relation to commission sellers. The stallholders claim that they do not need the commission sellers, that they represent a drain on their margin of profit, and that they clutter and crowd the atmosphere of the market place. The commission sellers, in their turn, claim that they are an invaluable asset to the marketing system, that they help tourists find their way through a maze of merchandise in the market place, and that they entice tourists to buy when they might not otherwise do so. Although the *lèk* system allows those without stock-in-trade to still participate at some level in the market, profits from *lèk* are always small. The merchandise credit system, on the other hand, can be a much more lucrative form of trade in which those without stock-in-trade are also able to participate. For the purposes of clarity in presentation, I will divide merchandise credit arrangements into two different categories: market-place credit and client credit.

Market-place credit

Watching from a distance the transactions of a market-place buyer, a trader might notice that a customer is particularly interested in a certain type of merchandise (e.g., bronze figurines, Dan face masks, figural goldweights, ivory jewelry, etc.). Having observed the buyer's tastes and preferences, the trader may try to pursue the client with whatever it is s/he seems most to want. If the trader does not have in his stock the type of item which the buyer seeks or, as is more commonly the case, if he is not himself a stallholder and thus by extension not an owner of resale goods, the trader would attempt to obtain the object from another merchant in the market place. At the time that the piece is being "borrowed," the two traders must quickly negotiate a sale price which is offered on extremely short-term credit. Whatever the outcome of this rapid bargaining or price negotiation, the trader who pursues the client draws his profit by getting whatever he can above the owner's asking price. When a trader borrows an object in such a manner it is referred to as taking the object on *ràngu*.[31]

Prices set in this manner tend to be relatively high. Since the stallholder knows that the middleman has a potential buyer who is interested in a specific type of item, he sets the price higher than he might otherwise under different circumstances – e.g., if a customer just happened to pick up the item at his stall. Another reason for which the object-owner may wish to set a high price on the item is to discourage the trader from taking it. For reasons of social and commercial etiquette, a stallholder cannot refuse openly to give an object to another salesman (especially one of his own ethnic group). Yet, traders often have interpersonal conflicts which come between them and other market-place vendors. Although the trader cannot refuse to "lend" the object to another trader, he does have a right to set the price wherever he wishes – thus, the price can be so unreasonably high that the trader asking to take the object on *ràngu* could not possibly sell it for any sort of a profit. The result, of course, is the same as not giving the trader the item at all, yet the object-owner does not deviate from the ideal of proper commercial behavior which mandates inter-trader cooperation.

Client credit

In addition to merchandise credit which is set in the market place, traders also establish credit in the broader arena of urban clientship. Many stallholders, storehouse owners, and even some of the smaller scale vendors have a set of regular clients in Abidjan and other Ivoirian urban centers. Some of their clients are African art collectors or dealers, others are expatriates (embassy personnel, visiting university lecturers, school teachers, journalists, corporate representatives, lawyers, entrepreneurs, etc.) who purchase art on an occasional basis. Because the knowledge of customer location and buying preferences are carefully guarded by traders, most African art sellers have only a limited network of potential buyers.[32] The *ràngu* system allows a trader to broaden his pool of customers; while, at the same time, it allows the middlemen to retain control over the whereabouts and preferences of their specific clientele.

If a trader sees an object in the possession of another trader which he believes one of his clients may want to buy, he will approach the owner of the object and request to borrow it in order to show it to a prospective buyer. Commercial etiquette prohibits a trader from refusing to lend an object to a fellow trader. Often times, however, traders will have their reasons not to lend an object to a particular person. These reasons might include the middleman's reputation for not promptly returning unsold merchandise; his reputation for not having much success at selling merchandise; or his reputation for not promptly paying the owner for the merchandise which has been sold.[33] Since in the *ràngu* system of merchandise credit the risks are not shared between the contracting parties but are borne wholly by the supplier of the goods, the object-owner must be careful with the disbursement of his stock (cf. Geertz 1979: 134). Those who are reluctant to lend out their objects through the *ràngu* system resort to various strategies which are designed not to break the unwritten market rule that one must never turn down another trader's request for the temporary loan of an object. One such strategy is simply not to allow other traders to view certain items in one's stock. Some objects may be kept at home, others may be stored in sealed bags under the trader's stall, or locked in a wooden trunk at the back of the market place. When a trader shows an object to a customer in the market place, he may draw the customer aside to show the object in an area which is out of view from other traders. Although, to be sure, this technique is partly intended to convey to prospective buyers the impression that they are being shown something which is unusual and secret (and, therefore, presumably very valuable), the practice is also intended to prevent other traders from later requesting to borrow the object on *ràngu*. Another strategy which is used by traders in order to turn down politely a request for an object loan, is to set the price of the desired item so high that it would be impossible to resell it at a profit or even to sell it at all. This is the same strategy which is used to turn down a request for market-place credit (discussed above), however, in the case of client credit it is considered to be an even more effective technique. In the market place, since they are usually reselling to tourists with whom they have no long-term or repeated exchange, traders may elect to borrow an object even if the asking price is exceedingly high. Because they have no relationship at stake with the prospective buyer, it costs the trader nothing to try. With client *ràngu*, however, a trader is asking to borrow an object in order to show it to one of his regular customers. If the asking price is much too high, the trader may actually end up vexing his customer. The cost of this insult would usually outweigh the benefits of an unlikely sale.

One of the results of this complex interplay of credit and commissions is that when an item is sold the benefits are distributed among so many individuals that if the buyer tries to return the object it would be nearly impossible to recuperate the money from all the profit-takers and beneficiaries. One case from my fieldnotes may serve to illustrate the point. A French expatriate client bought a Dan wooden face mask from Kyauta Salihu, a Hausa trader at the Plateau market place in Abidjan. The buyer paid 70,000 CFA ($230). Later in the afternoon, on the same day of his purchase, the buyer asked for the return of his money in exchange for the mask. He explained to the merchant that he decided it was not worth the amount which he had paid, and that he had some doubts about the mask's quality and authenticity. Although he was one of Salihu's regular clients, the merchant was unable to return the money. Salihu explained to the buyer that the money had already been distributed among several people associated in various ways with the transaction. Some of those involved in the exchange had already left Abidjan. The buyer did not believe the trader's explanation, and as he marched off he told the trader that he would never conduct business with him ever again. As it turns out, however, the trader was being perfectly honest. The bulk of the money (wholesale cost) had been given to the two itinerant traders who had brought the mask, that very morning, to the Plateau market place. Another portion of the sum (*ràngu*) went to the stallholder whom the itinerant traders had first approached. Finally, a small percentage of the money (*lèk*) went to Salihu who had arranged, on behalf of the other stallholder, the sale of the item to his regular customer.[34]

3   An economy of words: bargaining and the social production of value

> The chief factor [Ogotemmêli] explained, in an exchange or sale is the spoken word, the words exchanged between the two parties, the discussion of the price. It is as if the cloth and the cowries were speaking. The goods come to an agreement with one another through the mouths of men.
>
> Marcel Griaule, *Conversations with Ogotemmêli* (1965) [1948]

> Value does not have its description branded on its forehead; it rather transforms every product of labour into a social hieroglyphic. Later on, men try to decipher the hieroglyphic, to get behind the secret of their own social product: for the characteristics which objects . . . have of being values is as much men's social product as their language.   Karl Marx, *Capital* (1867)

According to the literature in economic anthropology, bargaining is generally found in economies which are characterized by such features as a flexible price policy, the non-standardization of weights and measures, and the lack of a large-scale information network which serves to inform buyers and sellers about the current trends in a supply-and-demand situation. The bargaining process in the art market follows many of the same patterns as bargaining in other sectors of the West African market economy, and also shows many similarities to bargaining strategies found in market economies in other parts of the world (see Uchendu 1967; Cassady 1968; Khuri 1968; Geertz 1979; Alexander and Alexander 1987).[1]

The value of individual art objects is established in the African art market through intensive verbal bargaining or haggling over price. Bargaining is used by traders as a price-setting mechanism both for *buying* objects from itinerant suppliers or workshop artists and for *selling* objects to other traders, Western collectors and dealers, tourists or other buyers. The object's price depends on such variable factors as the source of the object, the prevalent market conditions, the trader's current financial situation, the time of day during which the sale takes place (or the week or month during which the transaction occurs), and the trader's personal relationship to the buyer. From the middleman's perspective, bargaining occurs at least twice in the "life history" of an object. The object is first purchased from the supplier through bargaining (Plate 15), and it is then sold to the collector or tourist through a similar bargaining process. More often than not, the price of an object is negotiated even more than twice – i.e., if it is lent out on credit or if it takes a circuitous path through the multiple networks of the market system (see Chapter 2).

In this chapter, I will examine the bargaining process which serves to establish the value of an African art object. I will draw a distinction between four types of bargaining mechanisms, which I will call extractive, wholesale, retail, and performative. Extractive bargaining is associated with the negotiation of *antiquités* (i.e., "antique" objects) directly from village-level owners.[2] Rather than determine economic value, I will argue that this type of bargaining aims primarily at coaxing the object away from its owner – luring an artifact from its indigenous milieu into the realm of the market economy, and thereby transferring an item from a non-commodity phase to that of a commodity. Wholesale bargaining is associated with the resale of these same items among the community of art traders themselves.[3] Here, economic worth is negotiated within the sphere of an African system of value. This type of bargaining also refers to the sale of newly carved objects – *copies* (replicas) and *nyama-nyama* (souvenirs) – from artisanal workshops to market-place or storehouse traders. Retail bargaining refers to the sale of objects by African traders to Western collectors or dealers. In this type of bargaining there is a tension between two different systems of value: an object's worth in the African trade relative to its worth in the Western market. Both parties in the bargaining transaction may be aware that two different systems of value are at play, and indeed both may be attempting to push the valuation process into the other person's domain. Performative bargaining refers to the sale of art objects by African traders to foreign tourists. This type of bargaining, I will argue, is at least in part a "staged" performance which fulfills certain expectations held by tourists concerning the experience of an "authentic" West African market place.

The four modes of bargaining exist simultaneously in an economic system which moves objects from one realm of value to the next. In the course of each transaction during the economic life history of an object which circulates in the African art market the value of an individual object doubles (at the very least) in price. Indeed, from the price paid in a village to the price at which it is sold in a New York or Paris gallery, the cost of an African object increases by a factor of ten or more (cf. Price 1989: 3). Thus, for example, a Dan mask acquired in a village in western Côte d'Ivoire by a mobile supplier may cost him $20 (in cash or barter equivalent). This value may increase to $40–60 when the item is sold to a stallholder or storehouse-owner in a nearby urban center (e.g., in Danané or Man). The price could then easily jump to $80–120 when the mask is sold to an African trader from the urban capital. From there, the object may be sold to an African dealer who intends to take the mask to Europe or America – he might pay anywhere from $200 to $400. The object would then

15 Hausa trader examining a Senufo statue before offering a price to an itinerant supplier. Aoussabougou, Korhogo, December 1987.

reach its penultimate destination in the hands of an American or European gallery owner who might pay somewhere between $800 and $1,000. Finally, it would be sold from the gallery to a private collector for about $1,600–2,000 (cf. Hersey 1982). As Abdurrahman Madu reflected:

A work of African art has no fixed price. I can buy a mask for 200,000 [CFA] and sell it to my friend Bernard for 300,000; Bernard could then sell it to Samir for 400,000; Samir could sell it to [the American dealer] David for 1 million, and David could sell it to someone in his gallery for 2 million, and so on. That's what happens; the price just keeps going up. (6/25/91)

The perceived value of an item is thus wholly dependent on where one is situated in the chain of economic transactions, and each transaction is characterized by the logic of its own system of value and mode of bargaining.

Extractive bargaining

In an edited volume entitled *The Social Life of Things*, Arjun Appadurai underscores the fluidity of economic commodities by demonstrating that certain items can move in and out of a commodity phase. "The commodity *candidacy* of things," writes Appadurai, "is less a temporal than a conceptual feature, and it refers to the standards and criteria (symbolic, classificatory, and moral) that define the exchangeability of things in any particular social and historical context" (1986: 13–14, original emphasis). In the West African art market, the commodity potential of *antiquités* is tapped by itinerant traders who travel from village to village looking for objects which can be transferred to the global economy of the art market. The fact that migrant or diaspora traders are largely responsible for the first step in the commoditization of African art agrees with Appadurai's general contention that foreigners are often responsible for major shifts in the definition of object value. "Dealings with strangers," he notes in the same essay, "might provide contexts for the commoditization of things that are otherwise protected from commoditization" (1986: 15). A Senegalese trader in the Plateau market place confirmed this hypothesis when he explained that prior to the Wolof commoditization of African art, Ivoirians had no idea that their artworks were worth any money. "It was only when we arrived," said Barane M'Bol, "that we showed them how much money their art was really worth. Now that we taught them this, however, they want to control the market and push us out" (10/26/87).

At the village level of the art trade, bargaining serves less as a means for extracting goods from the local context. The price (which is usually represented by the bartering of both cash *and* manufactured goods)[4] does not represent the "real" value of the object as perceived by either side in the transaction. To the seller, the price is a recompense for parting with a personal object. In the language of economics, one would say that the seller evaluates the object according to its use-value, while the buyer judges its worth according to its exchange-value.[5] Thus, in this sense, bargaining is aimed less at determining a universal price as it is at striking a compromise between two different evaluatory systems. Since much art is obtained during times of personal or regional crisis, objects are often sold as a last, desperate resort to obtain cash or its equivalent in bartered goods.[6] Some things which may be highly prized at the village level, may have no worth on the international art market; and, by the same token, other items which may be held in low esteem by village-level owners, may, in fact, be highly valued by foreign buyers. At this level of the trade, the bargaining has nothing to do either with what the seller paid *or* with what the seller knows about the "true" value of the object in the world market. Bargaining here is less concerned with price as it is with the negotiation of a sale – i.e., convincing someone to sell something. As Sekou Yaka once explained to me:

When buying in villages, you have to be very careful about what you say. You have to be gentle and polite. You have to explain to the elders that these objects are things which people want to learn about. "Your children," you must tell them, "won't be able to appreciate or understand these things unless we take them and preserve them in museums and in books."[7] (2/15/88)

Although the encroachment of Western demand allows for the possibility that all African art objects *could* become commodities, some items are never transferred to the economic realm. African art traders recount, with a tinge of bitterness, that villagers are sometimes unwilling to part with certain of their possessions. Malam Abubakar, for instance, a Hausa trader whom I interviewed on several occasions, told me about the time he spent traveling among the Lobi people in the region of Bouna in north-eastern Côte d'Ivoire and across the border into southern Burkina Faso. "I saw women there wearing ivory lip plugs and huge bracelets," he said. "But they wouldn't sell them for any price. It just makes you want to grab them right off their body . . . They didn't even understand what it was they were wearing" (2/23/88). To the women who wore them, these ornaments drew their meaning from the cultural world to which they belonged. They were, so to say, literally priceless. To the trader, who knew the value of these ornaments in the art market, the objects were meaningful only within the context of an economic world into which he hoped the objects could be drawn.[8] I asked another art trader, Abdurrahman Madu, how he felt about villagers who were reluctant to part with certain objects:

I think it's just crazy because they say they can't see themselves accepting money in exchange for something they inherited . . . That's the mentality of the villagers. Even if they're not doing anything with it, they would rather let the termites eat it up [*le bouffer*] rather than sell it. Even though it would be better for them to accept even just 1000 CFA with which they could buy some soap for washing their children's clothes, they would prefer to watch these things turn into dust. That's their mentality. (6/25/91)

Wholesale bargaining

Wholesale bargaining occurs among African suppliers and traders. It is a system of bargaining where prices are negotiated within a relatively closed universe of value (Plate 16). At this level, in the commerce of *antiquités*, the bargaining process does not take into account the value of the object in the village context, nor does it consider directly the ultimate value of the object in the West. Wholesale bargaining is rather a means by which price is established within the parameters of local standards and regional fluctuations of supply and demand. Although urban buyers may be more aware than their rural suppliers of what an object may be worth in the Western market,[9] they do not allow this knowledge to permeate the negotiation of price. The process of verbal bargaining is aimed strictly at determining a value which enables the seller to draw a reasonable margin of profit above his cost. This type of intra-trade bargaining is what comes closest to typical patterns of market-place bargaining in other sectors of the West African economy.

In contrast to the trade in *antiquités* – where bargaining is intended to assign a specific economic value to an art object – in the *copies* and *nyama-nyama* trades, wholesale bargaining serves principally as a means of product allocation.[10] Because many trade pieces are relatively standardized and substitutable, quality is more-or-less predictable and prices are generally well known. Whatever variations exist in prices are due to the relative merit of one artist's work over another's, or to the higher standards of one workshop's output over any other's. Since the prices of standardized goods are relatively fixed, whatever bargaining occurs at this level is achieved within a narrow price range. Traders are familiar with the "going rate" on any particular type of item. Therefore, any increase in price is a result of competition among traders to secure a desired lot of goods or a result of sudden increase in demand; conversely any decrease in price is a result of the middleman's need for immediate cash or the result of a sudden drop in demand.[11] By contrast, in the buying and selling of *antiquités*, quality is always highly heterogeneous, unstandardized, and unpredictable. Buyers can never be sure whether or not an object is "real" or "fake" (see Chapter 5). There is always a suspicion that the seller is trying to misrepresent the objects which he is selling. Thus in the transaction of *antiquités* there is always an information asymmetry between the seller, who passes on something uncertain (objects) in return for something certain (money), and the buyer, who does the reverse. Hence, in this context, to borrow Geertz's language (1979), the person who is passing on goods in return for money is far more certain of what he receives than the person who is passing on money in return for goods.

Retail bargaining

The negotiation of price which occurs between African traders and Western dealers or collectors is referred to here as retail bargaining. I distinguish this type of bargaining from the intra-trade negotiations which occur among African merchants themselves. Unlike most forms of wholesale bargaining, retail bargaining begins to take into account the value of the object in the West – i.e., a completely different system of valuation from that which characterizes both village-market and market-market transactions. While wholesale bargaining constructs value from local criteria of supply and demand, retail bargaining constructs value on the basis of Western taste and preferences. Dan face masks and Baule female figures, to choose two well-known examples, have historically been more valued in the Western art market than, say, Lobi statues (which have only been growing in popularity during the past several years).[12] Although the costs of extraction (by which I mean collection, transportation, etc.) may be the same for all of these objects, or may perhaps even be greater for the latter set of items, the Western market does not determine value according to supply-side criteria. As one gallery owner in New York told me,

16 Hausa traders bargaining in a storehouse. Treichville quarter, Abidjan, June 1991.

"What you pay over there, has nothing to do with how you price it in the gallery" (8/5/89). Thus in retail bargaining there is always a tension between two different systems of value. On the one hand, there is the African trade value (which is based on local supply and only a fragmentary or elliptical knowledge of Western demand). And, on the other hand, there is the Western trade value (which is based on gallery prices, auction records, and taste-setting trends). In retail bargaining, where there is a bilateral asymmetry between the urban African trader and the foreign buyer, the transaction is aimed at gauging the worth of an object in terms of the "opponent's" value system: i.e., how much can the seller get away with asking, and how little can the buyer pay. The use of bargaining as a method to overcome indeterminacy in a transcultural economic exchange was clearly explained in the early years of this century to a British traveler in Cairo, who reported a trader's response to his inquiry regarding how a trader could sell an object for two pounds for which he had begun by asking over a hundred:

These things [he said] are worth to us – nothing. To you they are worth various sums of money. How are we to know what they are worth to you? The price you will pay seems to us to depend, not on the things, but on the persons who buy them. You say this thing is worth two pounds to you. It might be worth two hundred to someone else. How are we to tell what it will fetch except by trying? (Conway 1914: 64)

One way in which an African trader can attempt to catch a glimpse of an object's value in the Western market is to insist that the Western collector or dealer open the bargaining process by proposing an initial price. I have witnessed several instances in which the seller was so uncertain of an object's value that he refused to bargain unless the buyer stated an initial price. When the buyer is not willing to initiate the negotiation (which happens quite often), the sale can be aborted by the trader, who would rather lose an opportunity to sell than agree on a price which he later finds out was too low. The same British traveler in Cairo reports another incident which neatly captures a situation where the sale of an artifact was thwarted simply because the buyer was unwilling to state an initial price. Because the passage demonstrates so clearly the interaction between buyer and seller in a situation where the market value of an object is unknown to both parties in the transaction, I quote the passage at length.

Someone must have quickly marked me down as a greedy collector . . . for late in one of the first evenings after our arrival, I was told that two natives were enquiring for me. They entered my room like conspirators, bringing an air of mystery with them. After seeming to assure themselves that they were not overlooked, one of them drew a small packet from his bosom and placed in my hands a most beautiful little manuscript of the Koran. It was fifteenth-century work, still in its original binding, and I think they intended me to believe that it had been stolen, as was probably the fact. It was the first time I had had dealings with an Oriental. Would that that lost opportunity might return!

But such a chance will never again be mine. "What will you give us for this?" they demanded. "We must sell it quickly, and you can have it cheap." I bade them name their price, but they hung back. "Tell us what you will pay; it is worth much more money than we can wait to get. Buy it from us, and you shall have it cheap." "No!" I replied. "I can't be buyer and seller too. Name your price, and if I can afford it I will buy. But I am sure this thing is too expensive for me." "A price, a price!" they cried. "Name a price that you will pay, and let us see." But I would not, thinking that they would only laugh if I did; so at last they suggested eighty pounds. "That is truly very cheap," I said, "and the book is worth much more; but I have not eighty pounds to spare, as I want to buy ancient Egyptian things, so you must find another purchaser." "We will take less. Tell us what you will pay. Name any sum." But I foolishly would not. Five pounds was in the back of my mind, and I was ashamed to utter the words. I refused to deal, and sent them away still urging, and finally whining out the words, "Name a price; name a price, however small." If I had said five pounds, I now know that they would have jumped at the money, and that wonderful book would have been mine; but through shamefacedness at a first contact with these new folk I lost a golden opportunity. (Conway 1914: 62–64)

Although, in retail bargaining the Western buyer is generally at an advantage in knowing the potential resale value of an object in the Western market, there are certain conditions under which the trader can manipulate buyer–seller asymmetry to his advantage: (1) when dealing with absolute one-of-a-kind objects; and (2) when providing a client with a regular supply of hard-to-find goods. If a work of art is viewed as aesthetically unique, with no substitutes, the seller has a great deal of control over the price. That is to say, since there are no other sellers of that particular type of good, the seller is not limited in any way by values established by his competition. As Constance Bates concluded in a study of the international art market in the West, the "amount of seller control is inversely related to the consumer's perceived alternatives" (1979: 170). Under these conditions, the seller can orchestrate the bargaining process so as to push the buyer(s) in a direction which may lead them to reveal what they genuinely believe the object to be worth – e.g., the seller can stick to a very high price in order to judge (perhaps from the buyer's facial expression or from the pace of bargaining itself) how high the buyer is really willing to go.[13]

In situations where a trader has a regular relationship with a buyer, he can often regulate his prices within a narrow inflationary scale. One case from my fieldnotes may serve to illustrate the way in which price fluctuations occur even within the marketing of almost identical items. Alhadji Amadou, a stall-holder at the Plateau market place, has a regular client who purchases Akan brass or silver spoons (*saawa*) which were used in the past for measuring and dispensing golddust. Although these spoons are not especially rare, there is a limited supply of the finest quality, oldest spoons. Since most itinerant suppliers knew that Amadou purchased these type of spoons, they would usually reserve their supply for him. Thus, within the Abidjan market, one could say that Amadou controlled a considerable monopoly on a limited supply of *saawa* spoons. His client would buy these spoons in small wholesale quantities of about five to twenty at a time. Amadou brought spoons to her home about twice a month. The client would select the best spoons from the lot. And with these, she would create box frames with displays of one or two spoons in each (see the discussion of frames and framing in Chapter 5). The gallery owner purchased the spoons for about 1,500 CFA ($5) each. In turn, she sold the frames (*encadrements*) in her gallery for about 30,000–120,000 CFA ($100–400) each.

Although Amadou had established an average price for the spoons (during the two years or so since he had been selling them to her), when times were especially hard he would sometimes try to get more money by telling the customer that a particular lot of spoons did not belong to him, but that they had been taken on credit (*ràngu*) from another trader who was asking for a higher price. Or, employing a slightly different tactic, he would say that the supply of spoons had been getting scarcer, and that the village-level suppliers were asking for more money. Or, taking yet another approach, he would insist that *these* spoons were not exactly the same as the ones she had bought before (*c'est pas la même chose*). In all three instances, the trader used these explanations as a means of pushing the client to pay a slightly higher amount each time he went to deliver a supply of spoons.[14] Sometimes the buyer would give in to the inflation in price, other times she would argue with the trader in order to have the price remain the same. Amadou was careful not to annoy the buyer. He would always try to push the price just to the point where he felt she would not argue too much. Indeed, the capacity to judge the consumer's spending limit is perhaps one of the most important elements in a seller's successful bargaining strategy.

On one occasion, while I was present in the gallery, the buyer grew irritated with the trader's insistence on a higher price. Amadou had a number of debts to repay, business had been bad of late, and he was trying to push the buyer beyond the point where he might normally have stopped. Rankled by Amadou's pressure, the gallery owner barked, "Why do you want more money for these things anyway? I know you all find these things for free in the gutters [*égouts*] of Treichville" (5/2/88). The buyer's comment raises an interesting assumption, which I believe is rather prevalent among Western purchasers, namely that the middlemen pay nothing or next to nothing for the items they sell. Although it is true that the cost of the object at this level of the trade is minimal in contrast to the prices which are paid on the final consumption side of the market, it is certainly not true that the middlemen get the objects for free. Indeed, the African merchant's margin of profit is far lower than the European gallery owner's margin. And the sum spent to acquire objects is far higher – when viewed as relative to annual income and capital endowment – on the African side of the trade than it is on the European side.

Bargaining as performance

In their ethnography of rural market places in Mexico, Bronislaw Malinowski and Julio de la Fuente tried to correct a prevalent view that market places in the non-Western world functioned principally as arenas for social gathering where people congregated for fun and carried out irrational economic behavior (i.e., bargaining). "We soon discovered," they wrote in 1957, "that the Indians or peasants never go [to the market place] to amuse themselves or for any other collateral reason. They go to the market to transact business" (1985 ed.: 68). Commenting further on the bargaining process itself, they concluded, "people do not bargain . . . for the pleasure of verbal interchange or any other psychological reason, but because throughout a market day the price of maize rises and falls . . . in a manner which is definitely determined by the need of the consumer and the financial requirements of the producer" (1985 ed.: 138).[15]

Bargaining in the tourist art market goes against what Malinowski and de la Fuente observed in the Mexican market place. Unlike other areas of the art market which do indeed follow a pattern of serious economic negotiation, the bargaining process between Western tourists and African traders is constructed in such a way so as to satisfy the image of amusement which characterizes the Western stereotype of market-place transacting. As one Western observer put it in a brochure distributed to American Embassy personnel in Abidjan, "Disputing prices and quality are part of the fun . . . and disappointed is the merchant who receives his initial, most often outrageously high, asking price" (Anon. n.d.b: 8). Or, as another Western buyer put it, "Most fun was shopping at the huts along the road . . . I always think ethnic jewelry and bags are very valid for spring . . . and I love to bargain; it's a real challenge" (Anon. 1984: 4). Commenting more critically on the issue, Daniel Boorstin once observed: "Shopping, like tipping, is one of the few activities remaining for the tourist. It is a chink in the wall of prearrangements which separates him from the country he visits. No wonder he finds it exciting. When he shops he actually encounters natives, negotiates in their strange language, and discovers the local business etiquette" (1962: 92).

Acutely aware of this type of expectation, African traders manipulate the bargaining process in order to satisfy what they perceive as the Western image of market-place bargaining. In so doing, they will exaggerate their response to an offered price, extend the bargaining time beyond its practical length, and in general use the bargaining process as an arena for entertaining the client with outlandish claims and humorous remarks – thereby blurring, as it were, the usual distinction between acting and *trans*acting. As Asan Diop, a Wolof trader in the Plateau market place, put it, "White people like to discuss the price for a long time. They like to be grabbed and pulled here and there. I know that's why they come here" (11/15/87). When bargaining with tourists, traders discuss not only the price of an object but also "sell" the object by introducing into the discourse of bargaining a kind of on-going product advertisement. The advertisement (by which I mean any type of discourse which increases the likelihood of sale) may include information about the object's putative collection history, as well as the symbolic meaning or traditional use of the object in its indigenous setting. It may also consist of statements about other types of people who buy similar items, or it may attempt to flatter the buyers by complimenting them on their good taste and aesthetic judgment.[16]

Hence, although on the surface it would appear that wholesale bargaining among traders and retail bargaining between African traders and Western dealers or collectors is the same as the bargaining which occurs between market-place traders and foreign tourists, the latter, I would argue, is a totally unique form of bargaining which bears only surface resemblances to the other forms of price negotiation.[17] Bargaining with tourists differs from retail bargaining not only in the sense that it is performative, but also in so far as the asymmetry between buyer and seller is *reversed*. While in retail bargaining the buyer has more knowledge of an object's ultimate value than does the seller (i.e., the Western buyer has greater access than does the trader to information concerning Western-appraised value), in bargaining with a tourist the seller has the advantage of knowing better what an object is "really" worth.[18] On the whole, tourists are also at a disadvantage in the sense that they are not familiar with the conventions of market-place bargaining. They may, for example, be unaware that bids must alternate in fairly rapid succession, that backward moves are forbidden, that accepted bids must be honored, that one ought not to break off an interchange that is moving actively ahead, and so on.[19]

One example from my field data, which is typical of many similar instances, may serve to illustrate a pattern of miscommunication between tourist and trader. A European tourist walking through the Plateau market place stopped at a covered stall and picked up an item from one of the shelves. She examined the object and asked the trader how much he wanted for it. Rather than simply state a price (as the tourist probably expected the trader to do), the trader began with a lengthy explanation of what the item was; he then looked around at other items surrounding the one which the tourist had selected and then scrutinized the object itself. All of these activities are means by which the trader postpones his answer about the price of the object, in order to give himself enough time to calculate his initial asking price – a calculation which is based on such diverse factors as cost, inventory status, time of day, month in the year, perception of customer taste, and the appearance of the client (i.e., as in the

French expression, *donner le prix à la tête du client*). After being told a price, the tourist put down the item. She then immediately picked up another object, and again asked the trader how much it was. Rather than state another price, the trader grabbed the first object and handed it to the reluctant buyer. She tried to put the object down but her efforts were blocked by the trader who now stood between her and the stall. He asked her how much she was willing to pay. The tourist insisted that she was only "curious" about the price; she really did not want to buy that particular item. As if ignoring the buyer's last statement, the trader offered a lower price. The tourist protested again that it was not a matter of money or cost but simply that she did not want to buy that particular item. "Alright," said the trader, "how much will you give?" (2/29/88).

The miscommunication between buyer and seller is based on the clash of two different understandings of the bargaining process. A knowledgeable African buyer would never pick something up simply to request for a price to be quoted in the abstract. The buyer would only select an item if s/he was interested in engaging in a serious bout of price negotiation. From the trader's perspective, the tourist, in this case, is attempting to gain market information without committing herself to buying an object. She is trying to overcome the indeterminacy of a market context where prices are not fixed or posted. An American expatriate once complained to me that she thought the traders did not understand the fact that people sometimes just want to "look at things." The traders, I would argue, are profoundly aware that not everything a person touches is necessarily something they want to buy; however, because of the way the market is organized the trader cannot know if the next item the tourist will "look at" will be from his stock or from the stock of one of his competitors (possibly located only a few inches away on the same shelf of the stall). Thus, it is to the trader's advantage to insist on selling the first thing that the tourist selects. I would postulate further that a trader's experience proves that with enough insistence a person may well be persuaded to buy something they do not initially want.[20]

Bargaining as social process

Beyond its obvious pragmatic function in establishing price, bargaining also plays a critical social role in the structuring of inter-personal relations within the market place. It provides a language through which buyer and seller create new bonds of solidarity where none may have existed before. When buying from itinerant suppliers, urban merchants interweave into the banter of their price-setting dialogue a socio-cultural discourse which draws on the language of kinship, religion, ethnicity, and personal history. Buyers and sellers often refer to one another as "brothers." If one is younger than the other, one may be referred to as "my son" and the other as "father." Fictive-kinship terms such as these are invoked either by the buyer in order to heighten his claim that the purchase price should be lowered, or by the seller to achieve the same goal with regard to raising the selling price. Islam is also often invoked as a common ground between buyers and sellers. This sort of appeal to shared religious belief was most noticeably used by a Lebanese dealer who bought from African suppliers. When a supplier entered the front gate of his estate, the Lebanese dealer would welcome the trader with the Arabic greeting *asàlaam àlaikùm*. Even though nothing else united the buyer and seller – neither ethnicity, nationality, class, nor economic status – the Arabic salutation was a subtle (yet, I would argue, calculated) way of communicating to the African trader that they had some shared beliefs and interests. Finally, traders will appeal to commerce itself as a "fraternal" link between buyer and seller. While making an argument to a European dealer for increasing his offering price, an African trader said, "Between us there is no difference. We are both the same" (12/7/87). The similarity to which the trader was referring was the fact that both he and the foreign buyer were professional merchants. By heightening the buyer's sensitivity to this shared ethos or occupational solidarity, the seller hoped to obtain a higher price (cf. Curtin 1984: 46–47).

A trader's initial asking price will vary depending on the type of customer with whom he is dealing. If the initial asking price is too low, the trader will risk having to go too near or even below his minimal selling price. By the same token, however, if his initial asking price is too high he may discourage not only the sale which is currently at hand but also all future sales as well (cf. Cassady 1968: 58). Thus, the seller's initial asking price must be carefully chosen in order to insure a reasonable margin of profit but not discourage or scare away the customer.[21]

An initial price is usually stated only after a protracted set of apologies and explanations. The trader's discourse is intended, at least in part, to stall his answer long enough to calculate his desired margin of profit (which represents the difference between his cost and his opening price – which usually must be at least double of what he actually hopes to receive). During the course of negotiation, a trader can also insert statements which (although seemingly superfluous to the price negotiation itself) are aimed at pushing the buyer toward making a higher offer. In order to deflect attention from himself and attempt to fix the selling price at a higher level than might otherwise be possible, I once heard a trader tell a buyer the following account: "The object which you have picked out does not belong to me. I am selling it for my brother[22] who wants 20,000 CFA for it. If it were up to me, of course, I would give you a better price. But since it is not mine, I have to sell it to you at the price he told me" (5/19/88). As the bargaining unfolds, the price will inevitably go lower than the fictive "owner's" asking price – this, after all, is in the very nature of the bargaining process itself. The seller, however, can stay faithful to the original script of his verbal drama by telling the buyer that he himself realizes that the owner's price is too high, and that he will tell the owner that he accepted a lower price because it was the only reasonable amount he could get for the object.

Another device which a trader can use as a bargaining strategy is to quote the price which he himself paid for a particular object. As a means of underscoring the veracity of what he is saying, when revealing the putative wholesale cost of an item, the trader will often accompany his statement by an invocation of Allah: i.e., "*Wàllahì* [in the name of God], I myself paid more than that for this object." The trader then follows by stating his putative cost. This step in the bargaining process has at least two effects. First, it makes it seem as though the trader is being completely honest with the prospective buyer; that he is breaking an unwritten rule of commercial competition by taking the buyer into his confidence and unmasking the seller's buying price – one of the most guarded secrets of the trade. Second, the statement exposes what would appear to be the trader's final price – that is to say, the lowest he is willing to go in this particular bout of price negotiation. Revealing cost (even if the amount is untrue)[23] is a radical move in the bargaining strategy. For, after a trader establishes that he has paid a certain price for an object, it is difficult for him to go below that price without jeopardizing his credibility. In order to make a sale, however, traders must often go below their stated "cost." In so doing, they will claim that it is worth taking a short-term loss in order to forge a long-term relationship with a client. They are thus able to turn a situation which potentially discredits their integrity into one which creates the illusion that they are willing to make a sacrifice for the sake of forging a union of commerce and a bond of friendship.

A different sort of price "ultimatum" which a trader can insert into the bargaining process is to say that a second buyer has offered more than what the present buyer is willing to pay, or simply that another buyer has offered a specific sum of money which is higher than what the present buyer has offered.[24] If a seller uses this tactic, but then agrees to sell the object for less than the "other buyer's" price, he can save himself from embarrassment by saying that although he could have made more money elsewhere he values his relationship to the customer more than he values money. By insinuating that someone else was willing to pay more, this type of bargaining tactic also lets the buyer believe that s/he is getting some sort of preferential price.[25] Since prices are not posted in the market place, there is no other way of suggesting to the buyer that s/he is getting a special discount off the "normal" selling price. However, by introducing a second (imaginary) buyer into the banter of bargaining, the trader creates the illusion that there is already an established price for the object, and that the buyer is purchasing the object for a price which is somewhere below that agreed upon value.[26]

Market information and bargaining

Knowledge or information is one of the most valuable commodities in the African art market. The importance of market knowledge was plainly underscored by K. E. Boulding when he remarked, "As it is exchange or potentiality of exchange or relevance to exchange that makes things commodities, one would think that economists would be interested in knowledge itself as a commodity. It is certainly something which is bought and sold" (1971: 22–23). With market knowledge, traders are able to have a better understanding of the buying and selling price of the objects they trade; they have a greater sense of supply and demand; they are more capable of recognizing quality and authenticity, as well as the fungibility and grading of object types; and they are better suited to predict future market trends – thereby being able to buy objects before their value increases and to sell before it declines.[27]

If market information were perfectly distributed, then there would be no need for bargaining – prices for all qualities of objects would be known to all participants in the trade. Knowledge, however, is not equally distributed in the market system. As Cassady notes in his article on bargaining in Mexico, "In traditional markets the vendor is not likely to have access to the type of market information that is routinely available through the newspaper or radio to those operating in markets in more advanced economies" (Cassady 1968: 59). And, as Geertz says in his essay on the Sefrou bazaar, information on the market place is

generally poor, scarce, maldistributed, inefficiently communicated, and intensely valued . . . The level of ignorance about everything from product quality and going prices to market possibilities and production costs is very high, and a great deal of the way in which the bazaar is organized and functions . . . can be interpreted as either an attempt to reduce such ignorance for someone, increase it for someone, or defend someone against it. (1979: 124–25)

Addressing himself to the case of the art trade in particular, one African art merchant, Abdurraham Madu, offered the following thoughts on the disparity of market knowledge:

You know that if everyone in the world were equally sophisticated, the world would chew itself up. We can't all have the same amount of intelligence . . . There will always be a certain number of ignorant people. There are those with their eyes open and those with their eyes closed. If we all had our eyes open – if you knew everything that I knew – things just wouldn't work. It's like a scale; as one end goes up, the other end necessarily must go back down . . . If everyone knew the same thing, then there would be no market. (6/25/91)

One of the key functions of bargaining, then, is to overcome indeterminacy in situations where only limited market information is available. Among the information which traders guard most closely there are three, in particular, which stand out as being among the most valued type of market knowledge: (1) price (both purchase and sale); (2) source (both village and intra-market); and (3) quality (whether an object is "real" or "fake").

No trader wants other market-place traders to know how much he has paid for any item in his stock, nor does he want anyone to know for how much he sold an item to either another trader or to a foreign buyer. When traders sell art objects to Western collectors or tourists in the market place, they often take the person aside so that other traders cannot overhear the prices which are being discussed. If it is not possible to move away from a group of traders, the seller might whisper prices into the buyer's ear (especially as the price negotiation reaches its conclusion). There are at least three explanations for why a merchant would want to tell the client his price in confidence. First, it is a dramatic technique which is calculated to let the client believe that s/he is getting such a good price that the trader would be embarrassed to have his rivals know that he was selling something so inexpensively. In fact, traders will even tell the buyer not to repeat the price to anyone else for fear that others will want to buy a similar item for the same low price ("This price is *only for you*"). A second motivation for stating the price in confidence, is in point of fact to discourage the consumer from repeating the purchase price – not, however, in fear of embarrassment for having underpriced an item, but in order for a trader to keep his financial affairs secret. If the seller owed money to another market-place trader, for example, he would not want that trader to find out that he had just earned enough cash to be able to pay him back. Finally, a third reason why a trader would try to keep his prices concealed is so that others cannot gain ("free") market information about the current rate on a certain type of item. Say, for example, that a trader sells a particular style of Senufo mask to a Western dealer for a considerable profit. The trader also knows that another stallholder in the market place has a very similar type of mask in his stock. The trader intends to get that object from the stallholder, and offer it for sale to the same dealer at his hotel later that day. If the other trader found out how much the foreign buyer had paid, he would either demand to receive that amount from the trader who took it on credit (*ràngu*), or he would attempt to find the buyer himself in order to sell the mask directly to him. If he is not aware of how much was paid, however, then the trader can try to get the mask for a lower credit price and make another worthwhile profit (from the same buyer) on the sale of the other mask.

A second area of market information which is highly guarded by African art traders is knowledge relating to the source of one's goods. No village-level supplier would want to let others know exactly where he was getting his art. Secrecy in these matters is the best way of minimizing competition. Once an object reaches an urban market place, traders continue to guard information concerning the source of an object – not from which village it comes but from which supplier or market-place trader is was taken on credit (*ràngu*). As part of the verbal exchange in bargaining, buyers will try to sense whether an object "belongs" to the seller, or whether it has been taken from someone else on credit. If the object is believed to have been taken on credit, then the prospective buyer may attempt to find the source. He may say, for instance, that he is not interested in the piece, and will then try to follow the merchant back to his supplier – even if this takes several days of research and inquiry. If the supplier is located, then the trader may try to buy the object directly from the source (thereby avoiding paying whatever profit would have gone to the additional middleman). If the object were purchased from the source, both buyer and seller would want to conduct the transaction in secrecy – insuring that the now-defunct middleman was not aware that he had been traced to his source, by-passed in the circuit of exchange, and shut out of his financial reward.

A third area of knowledge which is closely guarded by traders concerns the "authenticity" or "genuineness" of art objects. When buying and selling *antiquités* in the art market, there is always an element of suspicion as to whether the piece is "real" or "fake." Sometimes the seller knows if an object has been "faked,"[28] often, however, the seller himself is not really sure. Thus, the buyer must first ask himself, has the object been faked (by either an artist or a trader somewhere along the market network). And, second, he must ask himself, does the seller know whether or not the object has indeed been faked. What ensues in the bargaining process is a language game of discreet inquiries – in which the buyer tries not only to discover the "authenticity" of the object by examining its physical properties, but tries also to uncover something about an object's "genuine" worth by deciphering subtle cues (encoded in shifts in price and the pace of bargaining itself) which may communicate the seller's sincere convictions about the value of the object. If he felt that an object was fake, for instance, the seller might drop his price much more rapidly than if he had strong convictions that an object was real.

Discrepancy in market knowledge directly affects the price of exchanged goods. Those with a greater capacity to judge authenticity will tend to pay more for objects they believe to be of high quality (and, therefore, will have access to more goods). Those with a lesser ability to distinguish "real" from "fake," will tend to pay less (and, therefore, will have only limited access to goods). A useful model which may help to better explain this process can be inferred from George Akerlof's influential essay (1970) on market mechanisms in situations where there exists a high degree of quality uncertainty and frequent product misrepresentation. The example on which he chooses to build his model is the second-hand automobile market in the United States. In this type of market situation, there is a wide spectrum of commodities divided at either extreme between good cars and bad cars (which are commonly referred to as "lemons").

If the used car market became flooded with lemons, the result, Akerlof predicts, is that the price of *all* second-hand cars would be driven down. Because the purchaser cannot evaluate (with any degree of certainty) the"true" condition of a used car at the time of purchase (i.e., engine problems might not become apparent until some time after the sale was finalized), the reasonable buyer would offer the value of a lemon regardless of whether the car appeared to be in good condition or not. Hence, the seller of an average or above-average car is either faced with having to accept less than fair market value for the product he sells or not selling the car at all (Akerlof 1970: 489–92).

If one applies Akerlof's model to the African art market in Côte d'Ivoire, several parallels emerge. First, if one equates the category "good cars" with that of "genuine art," and "bad cars" with "fakes," one could postulate that if the African art market became flooded with fakes (as some might argue it already has), the price of *all* artworks (which are classified as *antiquités*) would go down. On the whole, this statement is true; however, for the African art market Akerlof's model becomes more enlightening if we append another dimension. Unlike the used car market where *nobody* can spot a lemon before making a purchase,[29] in the African art market some people do have the capacity to better recognize object authenticity. Therefore, rather than consisting of a homogenous class of buyers, the art market has a hierarchy of different buyers who can be ranked according to their expertise or their ability to distinguish "real" art from "fake" art. In expanding the applicability of Akerlof's model, I would suggest that if the art market became flooded with fakes, one portion of the buying population (in this case, I am especially referring to the population of African middlemen) would flourish while another would suffer. Merchants with less information or those with less experience in evaluating the quality of an object, would always offer the seller the price of a below-average piece (i.e., a fake or a *copie*). Thus a high quality object – which in resale to the Western art market would be judged authentic – would be purchased by the middleman for the price of a low quality item so as to minimize the risk of mistakenly overpaying for a portion of his stock. However, those with greater knowledge of object quality, would be willing to take bigger (informed) risks on the objects which they buy. This second group of buyers would come to monopolize the trade in *antiquités* – pushing out all those who did not possess a keen capacity to judge authenticity in an accurate manner. Competition, in this regard, is thus regulated by market information and differential access to specialized knowledge.

4   The political economy of ethnicity in a plural market

At the beginning of January 1988, after having been in the field for several months, I traveled with a Hausa trader to the town of Korhogo, located near the borders of Burkina Faso and Mali in northern Côte d'Ivoire. Korhogo is the largest town in that part of Côte d'Ivoire, and serves as a regional government center (*préfecture*), as well as the urban capital of the Senufo and Dioula, the two largest ethnic groups in the area.

One of the residential neighborhoods of Korhogo, called Aoussabougou, is inhabited largely by Hausa migrants.[1] Many of these migrants are traders or shopkeepers in and around Korhogo; some of them are merchants specializing in the art trade. In Aoussabougou, there are approximately six major art storehouses owned by heavily invested traders. Within the town of Korhogo as a whole, art is also sold from the street in front of the main tourist hotel, Le Mont Korhogo, and from a small stand on the veranda of the Motel Agip. Lining the hill in front of Le Mont Korhogo are twenty or so wooden tables with shelves upon which traders display their goods for sale to tourists. Although some of the items they sell are from the Senufo region, many of the objects are carved in styles which are representative of other parts of Côte d'Ivoire and West Africa as a whole. A number of the traders who sell in front of the hotel are Wolofs, a few of whom also own storehouses which are located in different areas of Korhogo.[2] Art is also sold in Korhogo by Senufo and Kulebele carvers from a cluster of family-operated workshops in what is known as Koko quarter.[3]

The trader with whom I traveled north from Abidjan, Abdurrahman Madu, is a thirty-year-old man whose father, about twenty-five years ago, made the transition from the transportation and marketing of kola nuts to the commerce in African art. After completing his Qur'anic education, Madu migrated to Abidjan in 1972 from his natal village in Niger in order to begin a career as a professional art trader. He started out by selling new ivory carvings, as well as ivory and malachite jewelry, at the Plateau market place in central Abidjan. At first, he was employed by his father as a helper and stall apprentice. Now, however, he runs his own stall, and largely supports both his ailing father, who still resides in Abidjan, and the rest of his family who live in Niger. Because

Madu is one of the most economically successful members of his family, his relatives (both near and distant) are often imposing on him to lend them money. On several occasions, he said, his penniless cousins from Niger have arrived by bus in Abidjan and brought the bus driver right up to Madu's home in order to collect the fare.

In 1981, Madu realized for the first time that there was more money to be made in the trade in *antiquités* than there was in the ivory and malachite crafts and other "tourist" carvings which he was then selling from his father's stall. While maintaining the stall in the front of the market place – where identical *copies* and *nyama-nyama* are lined side-by-side – Madu built himself a wooden trunk in the back of the market from which he hoped to sell older works of art (see Chapter 6).[4] He began buying stock from the various suppliers who sent art objects from the villages. Since he had already been working in the market for about nine years, he knew many of the merchants who supplied artifacts to the traders in Abidjan. From his earnings in the front of the market, Madu was able to finance the growth of his stock-in-trade for the trunk in the back of the market.[5] Over a period of about seven years, he has developed a small network of clients in Abidjan, and, at any given time, his trunk is usually filled to capacity with various kinds of works of art.

Before this trip to Korhogo, Madu had never been to the northern part of Côte d'Ivoire. However, he knew most of the Korhogo-based dealers from their visits to Abidjan. In fact, one of the most prosperous art dealers in Korhogo, Alhadji Usuman, is Madu's father's brother. While traveling to Korhogo, Madu said that he was not at all concerned with the fact that he had never been to the area to which we were going. "They are all Hausas," he said with confidence, "so there will be no problem" (1/20/88).

When we arrived in the town of Korhogo, we went directly to Aoussabougou, the largest Hausa residential neighborhood (*zango*) in Korhogo. We went first to greet Madu's uncle, Alhadji Usuman. He was sitting under the shade of a small storefront outside his family compound. His tall stature and broad frame filled the elegant scarlet robe that he wore. Madu and I spoke with Usuman for about half an hour.[6] The purpose of Madu's visit was never stated directly, but it must surely have been understood that he traveled to Korhogo in order to purchase works of art.[7] After visiting Usuman, we moved on to five more dealers all located within a short walking distance from Usuman's family compound and storehouse. All the dealers told Madu that they were pleased that he had finally made it to Korhogo. They welcomed him and hoped he would find something he would want to buy and take back to his market-place stall in Abidjan.

Alhadji Usuman is a wealthy man by any standard. His compound is the largest of all the compounds owned by art dealers in Aoussabougou. I was told that he owned not only his own extended family compound, but was also landlord of at least ten other compounds in the neighborhood. Usuman owns two cars, and employs a full-time driver. He has taken all five of his wives on the pilgrimage (*hadj*) to Mecca. He has borne the expense of several very costly cataract eye operations – a problem which now seriously impairs his vision. When breaking the fast at the end of the holy month of Ramadan, Usuman is known to sacrifice at least a dozen sheep. When *he* goes to Abidjan he does not travel the long and arduous eleven-hour drive – he flies Air Ivoire. Three rooms of his compound are used for the storage of art objects. Some of his more precious goods are also stored under his bed within the main family residence. Usuman has two full-time assistants who maintain the storehouse, purchase art from the Koko quarter workshops,[8] buy from itinerant suppliers, and sell to visiting African traders or art dealers from the West.

After several hours of making the appropriate rounds to greet all the major art dealers in Korhogo, we were approached cautiously by an old Hausa trader named Bagari Tanko. Madu had never before met this man. Tanko was an elderly trader who went by foot or, more usually, by motorbike through Senufo villages searching and bartering for objects of art. He had never been to Abidjan. Normally he would have no contact with Westerners, and, as a rule, he would have no business speaking directly with a trader from Abidjan (such as Madu). His normal network of contacts consisted rather of the established Korhogo-based dealers, such as Alhadji Usuman, to whom he would bring the goods that he found in the villages. Usuman, or one of his colleagues in Aoussabougou, would buy Tanko's goods and then transport them to Abidjan or else sell them to a trader like Madu who had made the journey to Korhogo. The fact that I was traveling with Madu was something of an anomaly to the traders. It is for this reason, I believe, that Tanko broke the normal hierarchy of the commercial circuit and approached Madu directly.

Tanko asked if Madu would be interested in looking at some old masks that a Senufo carver had just brought back from a village that very morning. Without hesitation, Madu agreed, and we followed Tanko to the home of Ngolo Coulibaly. Unlike our visits to the compounds of the Hausa traders, here our business was announced as soon as we entered the door. Tanko informed Coulibaly that Madu was an art trader from Abidjan who had come to Korhogo to buy works of art. He asked Coulibaly to show him the objects he had just brought back from the "bush" (*la brousse*). At first, the Senufo carver was reluctant to do so. He said he was tired, that he had just come back from a one-week trip through the villages, and that he would prefer to show the masks some other day.[9] After some extensive coaxing from Tanko, Coulibaly finally produced, from a vinyl travel bag, two small *kpélié*-style Senufo face masks (Plate 17).

Madu examined the masks closely – taking them out of the dimly lit room, and scrutinizing them in the scorching light of the midday sun. After carefully

17 Senufo *kpélié*-style mask. Wood with fiber attachment. Height 32 cm. Private collection. Photograph by Richard Meier.

looking them over and evaluating their quality with Tanko, Madu returned to the house, and asked the carver how much he wanted for them. The carver explained again that he had just returned from one week of travels through rural villages, that he had not even had a chance to wash himself or change his clothes, and that he would have consult with his older brother before he could state a price or begin to negotiate the sale of the masks. Tanko apologized profusely for not giving Coulibaly enough time to bathe, but he explained that Madu had come all the way from Abidjan, that he was interested in buying the masks, and, therefore, he really did not have time to wait around for Coulibaly to get his brother. Besides, Madu interjected, "you know yourself exactly how much you paid for the masks, so you should be able to establish a price without your brother's help" (1/21/88). The carver protested some more, but finally proposed that Madu pay 200,000 CFA ($650) for one of the masks (which was surmounted with a small carved bird) and 160,000 CFA ($525) for the other (which was surmounted with a geometric crest). Both Madu and Tanko exploded with laughter and then explained to the carver that although the masks he had found were very pretty and well carved, they were by no means old (*ancien*) nor, as the traders say, were they *top*. Madu would buy the masks, Tanko told the Senufo carver, because he knew someone in Abidjan who was interested in purchasing nice *copies* such as these, but Coulibaly must understand that these masks are not authentic, and that they are not worth anywhere near the price he quoted. Furthermore, Tanko explained, Madu was interested in buying the masks in order to establish a business relationship with the carver. Next time, if the carver found some *antiquités* or *top* masks, then they would be willing to discuss prices like the one he had just proposed. Without interrupting, Coulibaly listened politely to all that was being said. He then replied – with what can only be described as an air of mock deference – that he was not a professional art trader like Madu or Tanko, and, therefore, he did not know how to recognize the quality of art objects as well as they did. In spite of his limitations, however, he still thought the masks were old and therefore he wanted to get a price which he felt reflected their actual value: 180,000 CFA for one of them, and 140,000 CFA for the other.

The traders and the carver bargained intensely for a long period of time. When the negotiations were apparently not going too well, Madu and Tanko would stand up and step outside. Twice we walked out of the carver's compound, got into my car, drove about a hundred yards down the dirt road that led back to Korhogo, and then backed up to return Madu and Tanko to the bargaining process. After roughly two and a half hours of verbal negotiation, only 10,000 CFA separated Madu's offering price (25,000 CFA for each mask) from the carver's proposed selling price (35,000 CFA each). It seemed, for a moment, that neither would move on their "last" price, until Tanko, who had not said a word for some time, intervened in the price negotiation to suggest that the two parties compromise. "You both have made such great effort in nearly reaching an agreement," he said to Madu and Coulibaly, "it would be foolish to walk away now that so little money separates you. Why don't you each put in 5,000 CFA and be done with this affair." After much grumbling by Coulibaly, and yet another "staged" departure in my car, Madu finally bought the two masks for 30,000 CFA ($100) each. While driving away from the carver's compound, Tanko was thanked by Madu for his help, and promptly paid a percentage (1,000 CFA).

We returned with the masks to Aoussabougou. Almost immediately, Madu was approached by a number of Hausa traders – who, apparently, already knew what had happened at the carver's home – and was reprimanded in very strong terms for having bought directly from Ngolo Coulibaly. Alhadji Usuman, in particular, was outraged by Madu's actions. Usuman (who, as it turns out, was regularly supplied by Coulibaly) had not only been denied the opportunity to buy the *kpélié* masks, he had moreover missed the chance to resell them to Madu at a profit. Usuman said that the incident was especially insulting to him since it had been committed by his own brother's son.

Not long after the neighborhood was set in motion by our return, the Senufo carver, Ngolo Coulibaly, arrived on his motorbike followed by his older brother. The traders immediately stopped arguing and turned their attention in unison toward the two Senufo men. Coulibaly's brother approached the crowd of Hausa traders and explained to them that his little brother had done a very foolish thing. He was upset that Coulibaly had not consulted with him before selling the masks, since he felt that the masks were worth far more than Madu had paid. He requested that the masks be returned, and stretched out a bundle of bills in a gesture suggesting that he would give Madu his money back. All of a sudden, the community of traders who had just been quarreling so thunderously with Madu and Tanko, shifted their tone dramatically and began arguing with the carver and his older brother. Rallying their alliance with Madu, one of the art traders, Mamman Yayaji, explained in patronizing terms to the Senufo carvers, "A deal is a deal. If Coulibaly were a child then perhaps we would consider exchanging the masks for the money. But Coulibaly is hardly a child, he is, in fact, the head of a large family and a responsible husband and father. Therefore, there is no way we will return the masks." Usuman interjected, "This is not a serious way to conduct business. We are all here, after all, for the sake of commerce" (1/21/88). The discussion heated quickly into a verbal and physical dispute – Senufo and Hausa yelling at one another and pushing each other around. At this point the older brother said he was going to get the police in order to help settle the matter. The moment it was mentioned that the police might be brought in to resolve the altercation, Tanko interrupted to say that the real owner of the masks was the American. He pointed to me. Madu was only an agent that had negotiated the sale, Tanko explained to the Senufo brothers, so if they wanted to get the police it was with the American that they would have to present their claim. The masks were then abruptly shoved in my hands, at which point the Senufo brothers got back on their motorbikes and left Aoussabougou, saying that it was all an unfortunate misunderstanding but that they were willing to let the whole thing drop.[10]

As the community slowly calmed down after the event, two explanations were given as to why Coulibaly had come to make his claim, and, in particular, why his older brother had become involved. In their first explanation, some of the Hausa traders thought Coulibaly himself might have believed in earnest that he had made a mistake and sold the masks for too little money. He would have brought his brother along to add strength to his argument and to legitimate his claim. The second explanation which was given by other Hausa traders, which both Madu and Tanko thought was the more likely of the two, is that Coulibaly was expected to split the profit from the sale of the masks with his older brother, who was his business partner. Since the older brother had not been present during the transaction – because Madu and Tanko had been so insistent that the deal take place without the delay of getting the brother – he may indeed have suspected that Coulibaly was not telling the truth about the amount for which the masks had been sold. That is to say, he was questioning his rightful share of the profit. By contesting the sale in public, in the presence of the buyers and the other traders, Coulibaly's older brother was able to verify that the masks had indeed been sold for 30,000 CFA each (a figure that was mentioned several times in the argument, and which was the amount of money he held in his hand when he offered to return the sum to Madu). Thus, according to the second explanation, the Senufo brothers never had any intention of returning the money, taking back the masks, or even getting the police. Coulibaly's brother was simply verifying within the context of a public forum the details of a private transaction from which he felt he had been unfairly excluded.

The drama of the *kpélié* mask purchase in Korhogo provides a small window onto at least one aspect of the role of ethnicity in structuring the social organization of trade. The incident is not only a good example of an obvious shifting structural opposition – what Evans-Pritchard (1940) referred to in his classic formulation of the problem as the "fission and fusion" of political segmentary opposition[11] – but it is also a striking demonstration of the intensity of ethnic loyalty, which is (as we shall see below) a crucial element in the commercial success of migrant ethnic minorities.

Ethnicity and cross-cultural trade

Throughout the world it is common to find ethnic minorities playing prominent roles in, or even monopolizing, trade and other commercial activities. The

Chinese in Southeast Asia, the Asians in East Africa, the Syrians and Lebanese in North and West Africa, and the Jews in Medieval Europe provide some of the best documented examples (Cohen 1971; Foster 1974; Curtin 1984). African ethnic groups who have migrated to West Africa from other parts of the continent also play a crucial role in all aspects of trade and marketing. Among the best-known West African ethnic groups specializing in cross-cultural commerce are the Wolofs of Senegal, the Hausa of northern Nigeria and southern Niger, and the Dioula or Malinké of the western Sudan.[12] These groups have migrated throughout the globe, conducting their business – as ethnic minorities – in all parts of Africa, Europe, North America, and (more recently) Southeast Asia and Japan. All of these groups, not surprisingly, control major shares of the contemporary African art market.[13]

One of the reasons ethnic minorities play such a prominent role in trans-national commerce is that their alien status dismisses them from many of the social obligations or constraints which could potentially hinder the successful operation of economic exchange. If, for example, a trader were fully part of a village society and subject to the controls and moral obligations of the community, he would be expected to be generous in the "traditional way" to those in need. It would be difficult for him to refuse credit, for example, and it would not always be possible to collect debts. In short, it would be hard to reap a profit from the very network of kin, neighbors, and friends on whom a trader's life was dependent and with whom he was socially and culturally intermeshed (Bonacich 1973: 585; Foster 1974: 441).

Although ethnic minorities are involved, for different reasons, in a huge variety of commercial enterprises, a trader's status as an outsider is almost a necessary precondition for participating in the African art trade. If members of the local population attempted openly to buy and sell art objects on their own, they would inevitably face the scorn of the community. In many cases, they would probably be punished severely if they were found selling sacred objects.

As a means of diverting local outrage, village elders who are forced, by economic need, to sell sacred goods to traders often report to their community that the pieces were stolen by the traders. Traders say that as a result of this practice some itinerant merchants have even been killed by local populations. In one exceptional case with which I am familiar, a village community reported the theft of a mask to the local police. The matter was brought to authorities in Abidjan who were able to trace the mask to a Wolof trader who had already left for France with the object. The trader's associates in Abidjan were able to contact him in Paris before the mask had been sold, and the object was shipped back to Abidjan and returned to the village. The Wolof trader was never reimbursed for the cost of the mask, but he avoided a serious legal confron-tation (which he would almost surely have lost). This is the only widely reported instance of its kind. In this case, extensive media coverage and the Ivoirian government's recent campaign for nationalism through the preservation of local artistic traditions (see below) were largely responsible for the return of the sacred icon.

Outsiders in inter-ethnic commerce have the advantage of being able to leave an area quickly if they are caught in illicit or sacrilegious activities. Furthermore, they have the advantage of not being enmeshed in the moral or religious fabric of the local community with whom they trade. As Georg Simmel once put it, the itinerant trader, whose status in a community is defined as that of outsider or stranger, "is not tied down in his action by habit, piety, and precedent" (1950: 405; cf. Levine 1979). Abdurrahman Madu said:

In the past, most Ivoirians who came to the market place were afraid to touch the masks. They thought that they would die if they came in contact with them. To these people the masks were fetishes. For those of us who sell masks, however, we can touch them all we want. We don't give a damn. Even if they tell me that there's a certain kind of mask that prevents you from sleeping at night, I could take it home with me and use it as a pillow. Because I don't believe in these things. You have to believe in something in order for it to be effective. If you don't believe in it, then nothing will ever happen to you. (6/25/91)

Since a disproportionate number of art traders – whether they be Wolof, Hausa, or Mande – are Muslim in faith, their commercial activities are not hindered by conflicting ethical interests or religious beliefs. Immersed solely in the economics of the trade, Muslim traders are completely detached from the spiritual aspect of the objects they sell. As Alhadji Kabiru stated when discussing a Baule monkey figure (*asri kofi*) that was displayed in his stall: "To me this thing represents money. To the Baule it's a god. A Baule could die if he touched this. Yet to me it means absolutely nothing. It's simply a piece of wood – no different from this countertop [in my stall]. It means nothing to me . . . To me this is just money, it's not a fetish" (6/19/91).

Muslim traders have no interest in collecting the African art they sell. Most traders decorate their home with Western products – images of urban prosperity clipped from newspapers and magazines, wall calendars with glossy pin-ups, colorful posters, or banners supporting African and European sports teams. As Malam Yaaro stressed in one of our conversations, "If you see a Muslim selling [African] art, you can be sure there is a non-Muslim somewhere who is buying it. I would never spend money on art just to display it on a table . . . I wouldn't want my children to see it or to know anything about it" (6/22/91).

Indeed, many of the art traders are critical of the populations from whom they buy art – viewing them variously as pagan, idolatrous, animistic, and superstitious.[14] As Yaaro went on to say:

These people speak to their [art] objects but they never speak back. If you leave the object somewhere for a year or so, and then return, you'll find that it hasn't moved, it hasn't eaten, it hasn't drunk, it hasn't spoken. But if the object really were a god then it would speak back when spoken to! Only the people who don't yet know God worship things in this way. We Muslims have never done that. (6/22/91)

Both the Qur'an and the hadith[15] take a decidedly aniconic stance – a negative view toward representational art – and, in particular, both strongly condemn the creation of idols and their use in religious practice. "The hadith literature," René Bravmann notes, "is uncompromising on the subject of representational art, and its judgments are leveled not only at all types of image-makers – that is, painters and sculptors – but also at all types of artistic creativity in which representational forms are possible" (1974: 16). Since Islam strongly condemns the fashioning of representational art and the worship of figural forms, the activities of art traders should not only be seen as non-conflicting with their own religious beliefs, but indeed the decontextualization of sacred materials could actually be looked upon favorably by the religion of the traders.[16]

Situational ethnic identity

In his classic monograph *Political Systems of Highland Burma* (1954), Edmund Leach argued that ethnicity is based on subjective claims of categorical ascription that have no necessary relationship to an observer's perception of cultural discontinuities (cf. Bentley 1987). His argument can be interpreted as a direct challenge to socio-geographic models of "culture areas" – e.g., see Melville Herskovits (1930) on the mapping of ethnic groups in Africa – in which complexes of cultural traits that are identified by observers are used to map cultural or ethnic divisions within a prescribed geographic region. Subsequent to Leach's work on ethnicity and ethnic group identity, the culture area approach has largely fallen into disfavor among anthropologists. As Fredrik Barth concluded in his work among the Swat Pathan, "the concept of 'culture areas' . . . becomes inapplicable. Different ethnic groups and culture types will have overlapping distributions and disconforming borders" (1956: 1088).

The insight that ethnicity is claimed rather than predetermined (in some primordial way) has been widely adopted in social scientific studies of ethnic identity (Wallerstein 1960; Barth, ed. 1969; Skinner 1975; Schildkrout 1978; Van Binsbergen 1981; Maybury-Lewis 1984; Comaroff 1987; Moore 1989). Such studies view ethnicity variously as a conscious expression of short-term economic interest, as a fiction constructed by leaders and sold to their followers, or as the by-product of a dynamic process of interest aggregation. The departure from fixed ethnic attributes allows for the possibility of shifting ethnic identity according to situational circumstance. In the art trade, merchants manipulate their ethnic identity according to what they perceive as shifting economic advantage. Although, as noted earlier, many of the traders in the Plateau market place in Abidjan are Wolofs from Senegal they will often tell tourists that they are from Côte d'Ivoire and usually, more precisely, that they are Baule. Wolof traders claim to be from Côte d'Ivoire in order to satisfy the tourist's quest for authenticity. Traders say that tourists prefer to buy souvenirs from Ivoirian merchants – the authenticity of the experience being heightened if they buy from "local" or "native" sellers (cf. MacCannell 1976: 149–60). The reason many Wolofs claim specifically to be members of the Baule ethnic group is twofold. First, since much of the art that tourists buy is carved in the Baule style (e.g., wooden Baule face masks and statues), a trader's claim to Baule ethnicity makes him a more legitimate spokesman for the objects he sells. Second, since it is a well-known fact that the President of the Republic of Côte d'Ivoire, Félix Houphouët-Boigny, is of Baule heritage, by claiming Baule identity the trader is also drawing a symbolic connection between himself, the President, and the state. When making a sale, traders will sometimes make direct reference to the President. If they are trying to sell a Baule mask, for example, they might say, "This is a mask from the President's village." Or, when selling a Dan doll, I once overheard a trader telling a group of tourists, "These are [like] the dancers that came out to entertain the President. I saw them on television" (10/11/87). The practice of "ethnic prevarication" is so widespread in the market place, that even a popular Côte d'Ivoire guide book finds reason to warn tourists about the manipulation of national and ethnic identities: "[M]any of the Senegalese try to pass themselves off as Ivoirians in order to lend authority to their pittance of knowledge about Ivoirian art" (Rémy 1976: 89, my translation from the French).[17]

Traders who do not try to hide their Senegalese identity – i.e., those who admit openly to being Wolof – emphasize instead in the banter of bargaining their "pan-African" identity. Remarks of this nature include: "We are all Africans in the marketplace"; "We are all brothers"; "All Africans are the same." When I interviewed Mulinde Robert, a Nigerian merchant who now sells in the United States, I asked him why he became involved in the African art trade. He answered, succinctly, "Well first of all, I am African" (9/12/89).

The fabrics of identity

Because the authenticity of an African art object is often measured not only by the quality of the object itself but also by the characteristics (credibility, reputation, knowledge, appearance) of the person selling the object, African art dealers who have extensive contact with Western buyers sometimes choose their attire carefully in order to heighten or underscore their status as "authentic"